The HIGHLY EFFECTIVE TEACHER

Jeff C. Marshall is also the author of *Succeeding with Inquiry in Science and Math Classrooms* (ASCD)

ASCD MEMBER BOOK

Many ASCD members received this book as a
member benefit upon its initial release.

Learn more at: **www.ascd.org/memberbooks**

JEFF C. MARSHALL

The HIGHLY EFFECTIVE TEACHER

7 Classroom-Tested Practices That Foster Student Success

ASCD | Alexandria, VA USA

1703 N. Beauregard St. • Alexandria, VA 22311-1714 USA
Phone: 800-933-2723 or 703-578-9600 • Fax: 703-575-5400
Website: www.ascd.org • E-mail: member@ascd.org
Author guidelines: www.ascd.org/write

Deborah S. Delisle, *Executive Director;* Robert D. Clouse, *Managing Editor, Digital Content & Publications;* Stefani Roth, *Publisher;* Genny Ostertag, *Director, Content Acquisitions;* Allison Scott, *Acquisitions Editor;* Julie Houtz, *Director, Book Editing & Production;* Darcie Russell, *Editor;* Lindsey Smith, *Senior Graphic Designer;* Mike Kalyan, *Manager, Production Services;* Valerie Younkin, *Production Designer*

Material in this work is based upon the work supported by the National Science Foundation under Grant #DRL-0952160. Any opinions, findings, and conclusions or recommendations expressed in this material are those of the author and do not necessarily reflect the views of the National Science Foundation.

All referenced trademarks are the property of their respective owners.

All web links in this book are correct as of the publication date below but may have become inactive or otherwise modified since that time. If you notice a deactivated or changed link, please e-mail books@ascd.org with the words "Link Update" in the subject line. In your message, please specify the web link, the book title, and the page number on which the link appears.

PAPERBACK ISBN: 978-1-4166-2168-3   ASCD product #117001

PDF E-BOOK ISBN: 978-1-4166-2226-0 see Books in Print for other formats.

Quantity discounts: 10–49, 10%; 50+, 15%; 1,000+, special discounts (e-mail programteam@ascd.org or call 800-933-2723, ext. 5773, or 703-575-5773). For desk copies, go to www.ascd.org/deskcopy.

ASCD Member Book No. FY16-6B (Apr 2016 PS). ASCD Member Books mail to Premium (P), Select (S), and Institutional Plus (I+) members on this schedule: Jan, PSI+; Feb, P; Apr, PSI+; May, P; Jul, PSI+; Aug, P; Sep, PSI+; Nov, PSI+; Dec, P. For current details on membership, see www.ascd.org/membership.

Library of Congress Cataloging-in-Publication Data

Names: Marshall, Jeff C., 1965- author.
Title: The highly effective teacher : 7 classroom-tested practices that
   foster student success / Jeff C. Marshall.
Description: Alexandria, Virginia : ASCD, [2016] | Includes bibliographical
   references and index.
Identifiers: LCCN 2015048024 (print) | LCCN 2016006283 (ebook) | ISBN
   9781416621683 (pbk.) | ISBN 9781416622260 (PDF)
Subjects: LCSH: Effective teaching. | Classroom management.
Classification: LCC LB1025.3 .M337125 2016 (print) | LCC LB1025.3 (ebook) |
   DDC 371.102–dc23
LC record available at http://lccn.loc.gov/2015048024

25 24 23 22 21 20 19 18 17 16   1 2 3 4 5 6 7 8 9 10 11 12

The HIGHLY EFFECTIVE TEACHER

7 Classroom-Tested Practices That Foster Student Success

Acknowledgments

My desire to improve teaching and learning has existed for several decades. My wife, Wendy, and my children, Anna and Ben, are among my greatest inspirations. My children's curiosity about how the world works is fun to witness and is something that I desire to inspire in all. Further, my students continue to invigorate my thirst to know and understand how to best improve teaching and learning for all.

Additionally, I am deeply appreciative of the input and time contributed by Julie Smart and Danny Alston. Their research assistance in developing, testing, and validating TIPS has been immensely helpful in moving this book forward. Their questions posed and conversations engaged in helped make this book a better overall product for teachers and leaders.

Over the course of my professional career, many individuals have helped to influence my writing and insights. Dr. Ena Shelley, Dean of the College of Education at Butler University; Bob Horton and Mike Padilla, former colleagues at Clemson University; Doug Llewellyn, author and scholar; Chris White and Greg Lineweaver, classroom teachers; and scores of preservice and inservice teachers who continue to teach me something new about teaching and learning every day. This book would not have been possible without the willingness of hundreds of K–12 classroom teachers who welcomed me into their classrooms and engaged with me in conversations regarding their practice.

Finally, material in the work is based upon work supported by the National Science Foundation under Grant #DRL-0952160. Any opinions, findings, and conclusions or recommendations expressed in this material are those of the author and do not necessarily reflect the views of the National Science Foundation.

Preface

Educators are in a war that must be won. It rages in our schools every day, but we often forget what's at stake. Our opponents in this war include failure, hopelessness, disengagement, apathy, and despair. In addition to ourselves, the key players include our students, some of whose lives seem complicated beyond comprehension, characterized by daily struggles that are—to continue the analogy—like being in a war.

For those who consider these statements to be a bit melodramatic, I remind you that education is the key to future success, and if students fail, the possibilities that education affords them vanish. We shower accolades upon a select few in our schools, but what about the least, the lost, the failing, and the disengaged?

In all probability, if you are reading this book you are seeking solutions to these challenges but don't know how to best proceed. Although we as educators lack control over every element affecting a child's educational success, we do have tremendous influence over what transpires in our classrooms as we work with each child. My goal, both in my career and in this book, is to help teachers and educational leaders find opportunities to develop their abilities to help *all* students grow, achieve, and excel in ways that more appropriately align with each student's individual potential.

The book begins by acknowledging that we cannot solve everything that ails our students, their families, or the educational system as a whole.

It does, however, provide suggestions and strategies for dramatically improving student achievement and success. I begin with the premise that we can vastly improve the learning in our classrooms when we maximize our performance through intentional, effective instructional improvements. My work has consistently demonstrated that this is possible.

Simply put, this book provides a systematic way to study and analyze teacher effectiveness that is directly tied to student success. Specifically, it focuses on intentional, transformative actions that, when proficiently implemented, can move teachers from delivering learning experiences that are frequently perfunctory and ineffective to experiences that are highly engaging, fundamentally purposeful, and deeply thoughtful. Improving the intentionality of teaching can result in higher achievement and increased growth for all students.

My hope is that this book will inspire important conversations that can help you, your department, your school, or your district make significant strides toward improving intentionality of practice, with the goal of fostering greater student success. Effective teaching is neither simple nor easy, but when achieved, it is extremely rewarding for teacher and students alike.

Introduction

Let me begin by stating what this book is *not*. This book is *not* about adding another initiative to your already full platter; nor does it offer an untested gimmick or a quick fix that promises to solve everything that's wrong in your classroom.

Rather, it focuses on essential research-based, field-tested teacher actions that increase the likelihood of student success. These teacher actions are presented in the form of a teacher effectiveness measure—the Teacher Intentionality of Practice Scale, or TIPS—that can help guide you in your own transformations toward attaining proficiency and beyond. In addition, the book suggests professional development resources to help guide self-studies, building-level support, or district-level growth.

Perhaps you are already proficient in one or more of the seven essential aspects of teacher effectiveness highlighted in this book. If so, it is important to identify and celebrate these areas—and to continue to refine them. The primary goal then becomes to tackle one or more of the other aspects in which you currently lack proficiency. Every teacher—from novice to veteran—has something to gain from this book.

Many states are reworking the metrics used to assess teacher effectiveness because the vast majority of teachers, frequently nearly 100 percent of teachers, received "proficient" ratings or higher. The need to rework teacher effectiveness measures is exacerbated by the fact that learning and achievement are not where we want them to be. These claims are based on data released by individual state departments of education 2012–2014 that include Colorado, Pennsylvania, Massachusetts, and New York. The only logical conclusion is that these metrics are missing something substantial because we know that teacher effectiveness is a critical component of student achievement. More specifically, we know that when low performing students are placed with highly proficient teachers, the achievement gap can be substantially reduced while raising the success for all students.

Most teacher evaluation tools focus primarily on the foundational aspects of teaching and learning (e.g., planning, classroom management, instructional strategies) when determining teacher proficiency. Although straightforward, and perhaps easier to evaluate, the presence or absence of basic teaching skills (e.g., a standard or essential question clearly posted in the room) should not be our sole measure of effectiveness. Much more difficult to measure are things such as the effective use of scaffolding or the facilitation of meaningful discourse, but it is these aspects of instruction that are linked to critical differences among teachers in fostering student success, and they account for much of the difference between highly effective teachers and the rest (Marshall, Smart, & Alston, 2016).

The TIPS Framework

The Teacher Intentionality of Practice Scale incorporates basic factors of teaching and learning, but it goes beyond them by emphasizing transformative instructional practices (e.g., high expectations for all, increased creativity in the learning environment and in the instruction, higher quantity and quality of formative assessments, improved classroom interactions) that yield increased student success. The TIPS framework provides a reliable and valid measure of skills that distinguish proficient or exemplary teachers from less effective, developing teachers. Specifically, it comprises seven actionable areas that are linked to improved student outcomes:

- TIP 1: Coherent, Connected Learning Progression
- TIP 2: Strategies, Resources, and Technologies That Enhance Learning
- TIP 3: Safe, Respectful, Well-Organized Learning Environment

- TIP 4: Challenging, Rigorous Learning Experiences
- TIP 5: Interactive, Thoughtful Learning
- TIP 6: Creative, Problem-Solving Culture
- TIP 7: Monitoring, Assessment, and Feedback That Guide and Inform Instruction and Learning

TIPs 1 through 3 cover the foundational aspects of instructional effectiveness; 4 through 7 address the more challenging, though absolutely critical, factors.

Each TIP indicator includes a rubric to help guide teacher transformation, with descriptors provided for Level 1 (Needs Improvement), 3 (Proficient), and 5 (Exemplary). Levels 2 and 4 indicate the presence of components from both the levels above and below. All the rubric items are written and standardized so that Level 3 (Proficient) is the minimum target that all teachers should strive to achieve. Although some teachers are much closer to this goal than others, all teachers can attain proficiency and beyond with proper support and sufficient professional development.

How This Book Is Organized

The TIPS framework provides the core of this book. The chapter titled Needs Assessment helps readers identify their individual strengths and weaknesses and provides a professional development plan to help guide the desired transformations. The subsequent chapters explain a specific TIP and use a similar structure: (1) a TIP and its subcomponents, along with classroom examples, are discussed; (2) questions are included to prompt self-reflection, guide discussions, and promote deeper exploration and conversation around what proficiency looks like for each indicator (and subindicator) of the highlighted TIP. These questions are set in italic throughout the book as a reminder to pause, reflect, and discuss the ideas—and so that you can find them quickly when you want to refer to them again.

The goal is simple: improve teacher intentionality; something that is applicable to all grades and all disciplines of study. Each individual's journey will vary, but this book provides common themes, guiding questions, and proposed solutions to frequent challenges that teachers experience. Although difficult to achieve, attaining a level of proficiency or beyond in intentional teaching practices is well worth it when student success becomes evident.

Although some may choose to read this book from start to finish, I recommend a different approach, one in which individuals, teams, schools, or districts decide on specific areas (TIPs) they would like—or need—to target, and then commit to focusing deeply on those areas, moving on only after proficiency or above becomes the norm rather than the exception for that aspect of instructional practice. For most readers, the Needs Assessment chapter will help identify logical starting points. TIPs 1 through 3 may provide a good entry point for newer teachers or for districts or teachers that are reexamining their standards or curriculum. If proficient management is lacking (TIP 3), then achieving proficiency in other aspects, such as fostering rigorous, creative, problem-solving learning environments where high expectations are the norm, will be exceptionally difficult (TIPs 4 through 7).

Making a Difference with Intentional Teaching

As educators, we are bombarded with a vast list of things, the *what*, that we hope to accomplish by the end of the day or week. Perhaps focusing on the day-to-day minutiae without reminding ourselves of the *why* causes us to lose focus—straying from what is truly important to our students and us. Being intentional (in our time and effort) regarding our teaching practice goes beyond a myopic focus on such things as grading papers, answering e-mail messages, and calling parents. When we focus more on the *why* and thus the intentionality of our teaching, we begin to ask richer questions that guide our instruction, such as: How can I better engage the learners who appear to mentally check out? How can I make sure that my lessons are aligned so that the learning matches my goals/ objectives? How can I create a learning environment that challenges all while providing scaffolding for those who need it?

Excellent teaching is not an inherited skill. It demands intentional and persistent effort. The seven TIPs central to this book provide a realistic, nuanced framework to help move educators to the next level in their teaching. The TIPS framework scaffolds teacher improvement, and its descriptive rubrics articulate what teachers need to do to reach proficiency in each aspect of teaching and learning. Sustained reflection and study of individual practice begin to make a difference when teachers can back up their claims of performance with evidence (e.g., "I scaffolded learning by ____"; "High expectations were evident when ____"; "The following questions stimulated participation ____").

Each journey will be unique. The goal, however, is the same: devoting energy to research-based and classroom-tested action that make a difference in every classroom.

NEEDS ASSESSMENT

What Do You Need Most?

Just as we need to differentiate instruction to accommodate varying student needs, we need to personalize professional development to address varying teacher needs. This chapter provides an individual needs assessment along with recommendations to help guide the professional development of each teacher, department, school, or district.

I recommend that you take time to determine where your greatest needs are relative to the seven research-based, classroom-tested teacher actions highlighted in the following chapters. Collectively, all seven core indicators addressed by the TIPS (Teacher Intentionality of Practice Scale) framework provide a guide to significantly enhance the teaching and subsequent learning that occurs in your classroom. TIPS comprehensively and cohesively pulls together what we know regarding the intentional decisions that teachers make that result in improved student success. Using the framework may even provide the opportunity to let go of many nonessential components that your school or district has previously required.

The needs assessment found in this chapter is composed of 28 statements. You are asked to respond to four aspects associated with each of these statements: (1) the frequency of occurrence in your classroom, (2) your confidence relative to the statement, (3) the amount of evidence that you have to support your frequency and confidence claims, and (4) whether or not you believe that your students would support your claim. The scores are weighted as follows: frequency (50 percent), confidence (20 percent), evidence (20 percent), and student perspective

(10 percent). After you have completed the needs assessment, rank your total scores for each indicator (category) from 1 to 7, with 1 being your lowest score and 7 being your highest score.

The goal is to help you clarify your strengths and weaknesses, recognizing that we all have some of each. Specifically, the intent is for you to honestly and accurately report your perception for each statement. The column that asks you to reflect on the degree of evidence available is an attempt to align your perception with your actual, observable practice. Each statement is linked to a specific research-based, classroom-tested TIPS indicator.

Instead of recording your needs assessment responses directly in the book, download it from www.ascd.org/ASCD/pdf/books/marshall2016 .pdf. The password is marshall117001. The spreadsheet automatically tallies your results for each category. After completing the questionnaire, all you need to do is rank the items. You can then save, print, and share your answers. I recommend that you work with another teacher and have weekly discussions about your needs, your plans, and your growth. Or, if you prefer to work on your own, this chapter can help you establish professional goals for the next year or two.

On a broader scale, a department or a school can use the collective responses to spend professional development funds on the actual needs of the department or school, rather than acting on hunches or responding to sales pitches of unjustified needs. The results may lead a school to focus on one of the topics that most teachers agree is a weakness, or the school might focus on several topics, with each teacher targeting one or two areas of greatest need. We have known for years that just attending a one- or two-day professional development workshop or a single conference session will not improve teacher performance or student achievement—unless these experiences are situated in a sustained professional development effort that actively engages teachers in goals specific to their content or grade level (Banilower, Heck, & Weiss, 2007; Darling-Hammond, Chung Wei, Andree, Richardson, & Orphanos, 2009; Desimone, Porter, Garet, Yoon, & Birman, 2002; Marshall & Alston, 2014; Penuel, Fishman, Yamaguchi, & Gallagher, 2007). However, once the core needs are known and identified, then purposeful, sustained, and well-supported professional development can be created to move teachers, departments, and schools further along.

Using the TIPS Needs Assessment Instrument

The TIPS Needs Assessment appears on pages 10–12. Use the following key to score each item in the assessment:

Key for TIPS Needs Assessment

Frequency Score
0 = Never or very rarely
1 = Monthly
2 = Weekly
3 = Multiple times per week
4 = Daily or almost daily
5 = Multiple times per class or throughout class

Confidence Score
0 = Low confidence or not confident on topic
1 = Moderately confident on topic
2 = Highly confident on topic

Evidence Score
0 = No evidence to support frequency and confidence claim
1 = Some evidence to support frequency and confidence claim
2 = Multiple sources of evidence to support frequency and confidence claim

Student Support
0 = Students would not support my frequency and confidence claim
1 = Students would support my frequency and confidence claim

Rank
After completing the self-assessment, rank all of the total scores from 1 to 7, with 1 being the lowest and 7 being the highest.

After you have completed your rankings, identify which two TIPS indicators ranked lowest. These are the most appropriate areas to target first. The seven needs assessment clusters correspond to the following TIPs:

- TIP 1: Coherent, Connected Learning Progression
- TIP 2: Strategies, Resources, and Technologies That Enhance Learning
- TIP 3: Safe, Respectful, Well-Organized Learning Environment
- TIP 4: Challenging, Rigorous Learning Experiences
- TIP 5: Interactive, Thoughtful Learning
- TIP 6: Creative, Problem-Solving Culture
- TIP 7: Monitoring, Assessment, and Feedback That Guide and Inform Instruction and Learning

Needs Assessment Instrument

	Questions	Frequency Score 0–5	Confidence Score 0–2	Evidence Score 0–2	Student Support Score 0–1	Total	Rank
1a	My lessons are well aligned (standards, objectives, lesson/activities, and assessments are all clear, aligned, and well sequenced).						
1b	My lessons require students to engage with both process skills and content.						
1c	My lessons connect to other disciplines and within my discipline.						
1d	My lessons make connections to students' lives and the real world.						
					Total 1:		
2a	My students are actively engaged during instruction, and abstract ideas are tied to concrete experiences.						
2b	My instructional strategies are student centered (requiring more than mimicking or confirmation of what was modeled).						
2c	My materials and resources make abstract ideas concrete and visual.						
2d	My materials, resources, and strategies are purposeful, and technologies are transformative (allow student to do something not otherwise possible).						
					Total 2:		
3a	My pacing and transitions are efficient and smooth, and students respond promptly to cues.						
3b	Routines flow smoothly; my classroom almost appears to "run itself."						
3c	I convey a solid presence, positive affect, and patience with my students, and my students also engage in positive, respectful interactions.						
3d	I am approachable, supportive, and respectful during all interactions with students.						
					Total 3:		

Needs Assessment Instrument—(*continued*)

	Questions	Frequency Score 0–5	Confidence Score 0–2	Evidence Score 0–2	Student Support Score 0–1	Total	Rank
4a	I establish and communicate high, appropriate expectations for *all* students.						
4b	I model, and students demonstrate, persistence, perseverance, and self-monitoring.						
4c	I ensure that *all* students are appropriately challenged (regardless of ability).						
4d	I differentiate and scaffold learning for *all* learners based on varied levels of readiness.						
					Total 4:		
5a	I stimulate participation and involvement of all students throughout the lesson.						
5b	I facilitate conversational, engaging, and motivating interactions throughout the lesson.						
5c	My assignments and classroom interactions are purposeful and personal.						
5d	My students are challenged to explain, reason, justify, and critique responses of others.						
					Total 5:		
6a	I model creative approaches, and students are expected to find novel ways to communicate, share, present, and discuss ideas.						
6b	I create a culture of curiosity and questioning in my classroom.						
6c	My students are fairly self-directed and actively seek solutions to open-ended problems.						
6d	My students are expected to consider multiple perspectives or alternative solutions/explanations.						
					Total 6:		

Needs Assessment Instrument—(*continued*)

	Questions	Frequency Score 0–5	Confidence Score 0–2	Evidence Score 0–2	Student Support Score 0–1	Total	Rank
7a	I provide specific, focused feedback (not just confirmatory responses like "yes/no" or "correct").						
7b	I provide frequent feedback to scaffold learning.						
7c	I use formative assessments to inform instruction and learning.						
7d	I continually probe all students to determine prior knowledge and misconceptions.						
					Total 7:		

Recommended Next Steps

Although they are not absolutes, the following recommendations may help guide your next steps. If TIP 1, 2, or 3 is among your lowest rankings, then you should address these more fundamental pedagogical issues before moving to the other TIPS indicators. You are ready to move forward to another TIP only after you have consistently demonstrated and achieved proficiency. This accomplishment could take several months to a year or more, depending on whether you are seeking significant, sustained change and on the complexity associated with the intended change.

In districts or schools that have adopted new standards, new textbooks, or a new curriculum, it is imperative to spend sufficient time on TIP 1. Neglecting to support the transition to new standards or curriculum (including through the provision of targeted professional development) will result in teachers simply continuing to achieve the same teaching performance as in the past.

Proficient or exemplary performance in TIPs 4 through 7 is frequently what distinguishes good teachers from great teachers. Although every individual and every school has differing needs, preliminary trends from observational data from TIPS indicate that teachers' lowest areas of proficiency are found in TIP 7, TIP 6, and TIP 4, respectively. TIP 3, TIP 1, and TIP 5 are the areas of highest noted proficiency respectively. Remember that even though TIPS has been standardized so that the descriptive rubric for Level 3 details the expectation for a Proficient level of performance, teachers will vary in their proficiency among the various TIPS indicators. Don't feel the need to align with these more general findings from a sampling of K–12 teachers. However, the findings do provide a default context if you must work on your district's professional development needs with minimal input—and they may serve to confirm or refute what administrators and instructional coaches observe in their own buildings. Using a default is not my first recommendation because it does not allow for targeting actual needs identified or personalizing professional development.

The following chapters can begin to guide the analysis, the conversations, and the critical questions relative to each TIP. Please don't look at the ranking of TIPS indicators from the needs assessment in a dogmatic fashion. If scores are close, and if many individuals in the department or school have a similar need, then it may make sense to go with the group need over an individual need. The fact is that we all can probably grow further in each of the seven indicators, so you need to focus on where you can get the greatest return on your investment of time, energy, and school funds.

A few final suggestions may be helpful. First, proficiency in TIP 3 is a necessity. If you lack a safe, respectful, well-organized learning environment, then you will struggle to succeed with every other indicator. Second, TIP 7, which focuses heavily on formative assessments, is an area where fairly immediate changes can quickly result in improved student success. Third, TIP 6, which focuses on facilitating a creative, problem-solving culture, will be more challenging in some disciplines than others, but proficiency in this TIP is essential for living, working, and learning in the high-tech, modern world where students must learn how to do something purposeful with the information they have gathered, not just memorize and restate it. Finally, because many programs will want to delve deeper in their study of a given TIP, a list of resources is presented in Appendix B to guide further development toward proficiency and above for each TIPS indicator.

TIP 1

Coherent, Connected Learning Progression

Although it appears simple—teach a coherent lesson that flows logically—proficiency in this first TIP remains elusive to many teachers in their daily instructional practice. Yet effectiveness with this TIP is crucial to help build and support success with the other TIPs.

Far too often our schools and classrooms fall into patterns that can be described by an expression used by computer programmers and technology designers: "garbage in, garbage out" ("GIGO" for short). For computer programs or apps with poorly written code (garbage in), the outcome becomes a product that is unpredictable, that crashes, or that fails to achieve the desired goals (garbage out).

For educators, a lack of clear and focused intentionality about what we do and why we do it likewise results in poor and unpredictable outcomes that often fall far from our initial goals and targets. This chapter focuses on how to establish a framework for instruction and learning that is intentional—going well beyond a mentality that is limited to simply covering topics.

Have you ever noticed how two people may hold radically different perspectives even though the conditions appear virtually the same? Nowhere is this clearer than in the variety of perspectives that teachers and leaders have about the content standards adopted by their state. In a comparative study of exemplary versus experienced teachers, exemplary teachers tended to view standards as a framework to help guide their instructional decisions (Marshall, 2008). Experienced teachers, those with 10 or more years of experience who were not rated as exemplary, tended to view standards as obstacles or barriers that must be overcome.

Thus, one group sees standards as positive and supporting effective instruction, whereas the other views standards as negative and interfering with instruction. We can debate aspects of the Common Core State Standards (CCSS) for mathematics or English language arts, the Next Generation Science Standards (NGSS), the College, Career, and Civic Life Framework for Social Studies State Standards (C3 Framework), or standards adopted by individual states, but once the debate has concluded and the standards have been selected, it is up to the district, the school, or the teacher to decide how those standards will or will not influence the teaching and learning that occur.

One thing boldly stands out when comparing the latest iterations of national standards to their predecessors: expectations have been raised for all students. As I watch teachers and school districts adopt newer standards, I find that two attitudes tend to prevail. People in one group view the standards as inherently the same as previous iterations—thus holding on to what is familiar instead of seeing what has changed. People in the other group grasp and understand the change and actively explore how they and their students can succeed within the boundaries of these newer expectations. Obviously the expectations for each discipline cannot be fully generalized to all sets of standards, but the changes evident in many of the new standards include placing greater value on the expression of higher-order thinking (e.g., evidence-based claims, modeling complex ideas and phenomena). Although some excellent teachers have been doing some of these things for years, challenging students with higher-order thinking has become the required norm, not the exception demonstrated by a few teachers in each building.

Unlike many earlier sets of standards, the newer iterations help to provide explicit links between skills and practices and among disciplines. In mathematics, this means students must now focus on mathematical practices such as modeling solutions to complex real-world problems versus simply mimicking solutions to exercises that have previously been modeled by the teacher. In science, students need to model complex phenomena and justify claims using data instead of just making observations and listing terms. In social studies, students need to situate knowledge into a civically responsible context. For language arts, reading and communicating must be grounded in evidence.

The push for tackling complex thinking and supporting claims with evidence is now prevalent in all grades and all disciplines, moving students away from accepting an idea without challenging the thinking behind it. Previously, something such as "There is no right answer" was a common teacher statement intended to encourage student participation. The new standards suggest that perhaps a better statement is "Correct answers are those with solid evidence to support the claim." Note that in all cases, students still have to achieve the lower-order skills (remember, recall, list, memorize), but now such skills are a means to an end and not the end in itself.

The quandary and seeming contradiction for some teachers becomes this: How can we expect students to succeed under more demanding standards if they have not been successful with the previous, less demanding expectations? This chapter begins to resolve this tension, but an initial response is that perhaps the higher expectations will provide the impetus and opportunity needed for change *if* we capitalize on the opportunity before us.

TIP 1 focuses primarily on two questions: (1) How well does your lesson provide a coherent learning progression that unites both skills and knowledge (*Learning Progression*), and (2) How well, and where, is your lesson connected to both the student and to the bigger picture (*Connectedness of Learning*)?

Learning Progression

A vast difference exists between finding and teaching one of the millions of lessons available on virtually any topic versus constructing and facilitating a learning progression that is intentional, focused, and well aligned. For proficient teaching performance, the teacher must personally demonstrate and convey accuracy in the essential knowledge and skills; the lesson must be clear and logical in its progression; and it must be well aligned to the standards, objectives, and assessments. To ensure that the most appropriate lesson is selected from the millions available, we must be intentional regarding our choices. First, we must know what we want students to know and be able to do before we go chasing lessons that just fit a given topic. Second, the lesson needs to be developmentally and intellectually appropriate for our students. Finally, we must learn to tweak new or existing lessons to fit the needs of our students and not just copy and use as the author posted—particularly when it does not fully meet the needs of our learners or our targeted objectives.

TIP 1

Coherent, Connected Learning Progression

Score	1 (Needs Improvement)	3 (Proficient)	5 (Exemplary)
Learning Progression (1a)	**Implements sound, coherent learning progression.**		
	Lesson contains content errors, lacks clarity, and aligns poorly with standards, objectives, and assessments.	Lesson is generally clear, logically sequenced, and aligned well to standards, measurable objectives, and assessments. Content taught is accurate.	Lesson is consistently clear, logically sequenced, and aligned well to standards, measurable objectives, and assessments. Content taught is accurate and connected to the students.
	Lesson teaches processes/practices separately from concepts/content.	Lesson integrates practices/processes and knowledge.	Lesson requires students to engage with both processes/ practices and concepts/content.
Connectedness of Learning (1b)	**Connects learning to students' lives and big ideas.**		
	No explicit connection is made to big picture within discipline.	Learning is explicitly connected to the bigger picture within the discipline or to other disciplines.	Multiple connections are made throughout the lesson as to how lesson/concepts are connected to bigger picture within the discipline and/or other disciplines.
	No explicit connections are made to students' lives.	Connections are made to link content with students' lives or prior learning.	Connections are rich, vibrant, and linked to students' lives and prior learning. Students are actively involved in making real-world connections.

? *How do you know if your instruction is accurate?*

Teachers who understand their discipline and their content frequently convey an energetic and engaging tone that goes beyond just transferring knowledge to students. For years, educators have known how important it is to provide clarity of thought and purpose during lessons and assessments, but this is often easier said than done. Lack of clarity is often evident when students continually are confused about what is being asked of them or what they are supposed to be doing. Teachers often think their questions are clear—those asked both orally during class and on written tests; but this assumption is often challenged when students either respond with blank stares or perform worse than expected on assessments. Asking students which questions on a quiz or test were the most confusing—and why—is a quick way for the teacher to discern if the content was difficult or whether the wording was confusing.

? *What signs indicate that your lesson is clear, logically sequenced, and well aligned with the goals/objectives?*

A lesson must be well aligned. In proficient lessons, teachers make sure that the lesson activity or focus is matched to measurable objectives and that any assessments focus almost exclusively on measuring those objectives. For instance, if the 3rd grade science standard states that students will plan and conduct an investigation, then the measurable (and gradable) component becomes the degree to which students are able to demonstrate through their experiment the phenomena being tested.

I recently observed a middle school social studies class where students were tackling the following essential question: Were Hammurabi's laws just? (I will address the quality of the essential question later, but for now, let's go with the example.) This lesson required students to analyze the laws individually and as a class to determine their purpose and their effects on society. A subsequent quiz would ask students to provide evidence to support their claims.

Regardless of the objective or standard being addressed, the goal is the degree to which each student is able to demonstrate success. So it is fine for students to work collaboratively in small groups for a large portion of the learning experience, but it is important to make sure that competencies are individually demonstrated when possible and always tightly aligned with the objectives. If "comparing" is the targeted objective, then asking students to match and list on the quiz or test for the culminating experience would fall short of achieving the goal.

Even when the curriculum is prescribed at the school or district level, teachers play a significant role in how the curriculum fits with their students and within the learning context (past, present, and future). As I discuss later (TIP 5), the questioning and interactions used to guide the lesson help determine if the lesson becomes vibrant and alive for students, or if it flounders into an unpleasant and disengaging experience.

The integration of skills and knowledge—instead of being separate instructional components taught on different days—is one of the distinguishing features of CCSS, NGSS, C3 Framework, and most of the newer state standards. Although each discipline interprets this integration of skills and knowledge a bit differently, the essence is the same. In science, each performance expectation entails a combination of scientific and engineering practices (e.g., analyzing and interpreting data), core ideas (e.g., force and motion), and cross-cutting ideas (e.g., stability and change). In mathematics, standards are divided into mathematical practices (e.g., problem solving) and content (e.g., algebra). In social studies, the C3 Framework is composed of four core areas: developing questions and planning inquiries; applying disciplinary concepts and tools; evaluating sources using evidence; and communicating conclusions and taking informed action. In English language arts, the emphasis is now on processes (e.g., reading and composition) as well as content.

? *How do you integrate skills and knowledge when you and your students have previously only experienced them being taught in isolation?*

Connectedness of Learning

Reading a classic novel because it is important to be well read; learning to factor a quadratic equation because it will help in solving more complex problems; memorizing facts from the Periodic Table of Elements because knowing them will help later in chemistry; or learning where the key battles of World War II occurred because geography is important— these are all common yet trite explanations for relevance that lack the element of meaningfully and explicitly engaging the learner in the lesson. Further, many times the intentionality is lacking because the teacher either does not know why the students need to study "topic X" or there is a huge chasm between learning and the game of school that needs to be bridged.

Constructing a coherent and well-aligned instructional plan requires connecting learning in several ways to prevent it from being isolated and meaningless to students. The first critical connection involves linking the learning to students' lives or to their prior knowledge. Perhaps equally important is the need to connect the learning to the bigger picture within the discipline and to other disciplines. When learning is connected to the student and to the bigger picture, it becomes purposeful and valuable to the learner. Far too often learning lacks an explicit link to either of these.

? *How do you best connect the lesson to the bigger picture within the discipline and to other disciplines?*

In the earlier example involving Hammurabi's laws, students were using higher-order thinking skills, but the lesson had no relevance or personal connection to the learner. Students will never come to class asking to study the justness of Hammurabi's laws, so the teacher must provide the link or bridge to create a need or value for the learner. One example could include modifying the essential question to ask, Are all laws just? The lesson could begin by engaging students in a conversation or reflection on "laws" that exist in their home or an imaginary scenario about a legislative proposal to ban rap music for all individuals under age 18. Either topic could lead to a discussion as to whether a proposed law was just, effective, or good for society. Once students are engaged in the conversation and see a personal connection to the topic, then it is possible to focus more deeply on studying the concept in context, which, in the example of Hammurabi's laws, would involve looking at other cultures and societies.

? *Where do opportunities exist to connect today's lesson to your students' lives?*

Actions for TIP 1

To guide your discussions, self-reflection, and next steps, consider the following actions that address the central concepts for TIP 1: *Learning Progression* and *Connectedness of Learning*.

Action: Check Your Content Knowledge to Maximize Accuracy and Clarity

Most educators have probably not had their content knowledge thoroughly checked or questioned since they took their student-teaching content exams, such as the Praxis tests. To be clear, taking a course on the topic does not guarantee solid content knowledge, nor does it ensure an ability to link the content to other concepts. So you need to seek other ways to check the accuracy of your own knowledge.

One possibility is to get together with an expert to discuss the flow, content, and connections related to an upcoming unit. This conversation may lead to ideas for connecting the content to the bigger picture and for improving your depth of knowledge. Preparing several questions ahead of time will help guide the conversation. Consider these suggestions: X is a difficult concept to teach. How would you explain it to a novice? How is your work/field connected with other fields? What is new in the field?

If conversing with an expert is not possible (or if the very idea is intimidating), another way to help ensure greater accuracy is to study common misconceptions about the concept being studied. One misconception I have heard expressed many times by elementary through high school teachers is that the blood returning to the heart is blue. This notion continues to be perpetuated in classes every day, but a little research would quickly reveal that it is not true and would explain why the misconception commonly exists among teachers and students. In some cases, studying historical contexts will reveal how stories and interpretations have changed over time—sometimes making perceptions more accurate and sometimes, like the game of gossip, making them less accurate. In mathematics, you might consider common difficulties you notice in students' solutions to problems. In English, you could revisit common writing errors, along with recent changes in conventions used in writing.

A few semesters ago, one of my student teachers asked how she could improve her confidence as a teacher relative to her content knowledge. As this conversation proceeded, it was clear that even though this student had a 3.5 grade point average in secondary science education, she was uncomfortable connecting the key concepts within her own discipline. My response was simple: read, read, read. We can never be too well read in our field; there are always new insights to glean and knowledge to acquire. As you become better read in your field, much of the information will become redundant. At that point you can simply scan the material, staying alert for new points. Keep in mind that the abundance of resources available via the Internet comes with a caveat: millions of documents—including potential lessons or activities—are instantly available, yet there is no filter to ensure quality or accuracy.

Finally, another way to improve accuracy in your lessons is to invite a peer or department chair whom you respect to sit in on one or more of your classes and provide an honest assessment of the content knowledge you have displayed. You can then ask them for suggestions for improvement, where necessary.

We have long known that the clarity of the teacher is absolutely vital to maximizing learning (National Board for Professional Teaching Standards, 2006; Rosenshine & Furst, 1971). The ability of the teacher to plan and then implement a lesson with clarity is essential. The challenge is that we often assume that because we teach something, it is clear. Thus it is important to look for objective evidence that supports or refutes your level of clarity as a teacher for a given lesson. Questions are clear when students are not confused regarding what is being asked (this doesn't mean that they instantly know the answer, but that they are clear regarding the task at hand). If you have to continually reword questions for students, then clarity may be an issue. However, sometimes a question is very challenging and well stated but needs to be reworded to scaffold students' ability to answer. If students show knowledge and mastery in class and then bomb the test, one possible explanation may be the wording or clarity of the questions; or perhaps you were not clear about what students should know and be able to do before the test. Further, be careful when using tests or assessments generated by publishing companies; they are often overly complex or poorly written relative to your objectives.

Clarity does not mean simply telling students more; as other TIP indicators will show, clarity is often conveyed by how learning is facilitated—not just a clearer lecture or telling of information.

? *What steps can you take to ensure that you demonstrate, every day, better accuracy of content knowledge? Where are your lessons most clear/least clear? What is the evidence? How can you gradually improve clarity in areas of weakness?*

Action: Develop Well-Aligned Lessons

As I watch teachers deliver lessons or look at their written lesson plans, I often feel like I am watching one of those *Sesame Street* segments devoted to the idea that "one of these things is not like the others." That is, I notice frequent misalignment among the standards, the objectives, the lesson, and the assessments.

Making sure that all the lesson components are cohesively connected is particularly important with the newer standards. You may feel you are teaching a standard that is similar to an earlier one, but you may be missing the fact that a critical action verb has changed. Instead of being asked to *list* or *describe*, students may now need to *compare and contrast* or *calculate*. Changing the verb can change the whole focus of the lesson. Because the newer standards tend to promote higher-order thinking, you may frequently need to scaffold the lessons to the targeted expectation or standard, whereas in the past you could often teach in almost a direct match to the standard. For years, the work of Wiggins and McTighe (2005) has helped teachers, schools, and districts to adopt a backward-design model. This model seeks to ensure that the alignment focuses on the end goal. When you clearly identify what you want your students to know and be able to do at the end of the lesson or the unit, then you can work backward by asking what experiences are needed to frame the learning so that the goal is achieved.

? *Does your last lesson show alignment among the standards, objectives, lesson, and assessments? Do your test items reflect the standards/ objectives? For your last lesson, did students demonstrate the action verb (e.g., justify, evaluate, calculate, compare) specified in your objective(s)? If not, what is still necessary to get them to this level?*

Action: Use Essential Questions to Connect Learning

A well-crafted essential question helps frame the lesson by creating a connection to the bigger picture within the discipline, to something that is personally relevant to the student, and potentially to current events. If engaging students and linking to the bigger picture are the goals, then you need to frequently restate the essential question during class, and it is critical that it be well written and developed. Many sources are available to guide the writing of solid essential questions (see, for example, McTighe & Wiggins, 2013), but generally an excellent essential question includes the following criteria: (1) promotes inquiry and curiosity, (2) requires the consideration of multiple perspectives, (3) incorporates one or more major concepts or anchoring ideas, and (4) promotes deep critical analysis of ideas or data. As such, well-written essential questions are simple to understand (no difficult vocabulary or complex wording) while still encouraging rich discussions, deep thinking, and purposeful learning. Spanning multiple disciplines and multiple grade levels, the following are examples of essential questions (with the targeted disciplines):

- What makes a hero? (English, social studies)
- How can a business maximize profit? (economics, mathematics)
- What does it take to believe a scientific claim? (science)
- What is worth fighting for, and what is a fair way to fight? (social studies)
- When should we estimate and when should we be exact? (mathematics, science)
- When do the lines between fiction and truth become blurred? (English)
- How do we control a widespread contagious disease? (science)

? *What are three to five essential questions that you can use to guide the learning in your classroom during the next two to three weeks? What are the most difficult topics or concepts for your discipline/grade level? Working with others, brainstorm essential questions that can help to make these challenging topics seem more relevant.*

Action: Use the "Threshold Test" to Connect to Students

As you cross the threshold to your classroom each day, consider the following questions: How does this lesson relate to the bigger picture of your discipline? How does it relate to other disciplines? Is there a connection to current events? How does it relate to your students? If you struggle to answer at least one of these questions, then one of two things is likely occurring: (1) the topic or concept is a means to an end—it helps support further learning of other ideas or concepts later, or (2) this is an insignificant topic or concept and the need to teach it should be seriously questioned.

When learning is a means to an end, it is vital to continually think about where and how it fits within the bigger picture. It is not sufficient to tell students that addition will help with calculus later. Yes, that is an extreme example, but many connections teachers make are just as valueless and uninspiring to students. Rather, the lesson needs to be specific—to provide opportunities, for example, for students to engage with professionals (virtually or face-to-face), to engage with other students around the globe, or to post work on blogs or websites so that others can view or critique their ideas. In science, students could focus on sustainability issues that involve reducing their ecological footprint (Joyner & Marshall, in press). An elementary school might adopt a schoolwide theme of thinking like Da Vinci, with each grade level focusing on a different component of thought (e.g., observing, creating, seeing). In mathematics, problems could include more context; for instance, instead of solving 45 + 37, ask students, if Joan has $45 and Juan has $37, then how much do they have together? The first example is more abstract, and the second is more concrete. We have a tendency to start with the abstract and then make our application problems, if time allows, more concrete. It should always be the other way around. No context equals no meaning and no value.

? *What is the big-picture connection of today's lesson? What current events relate to your topic of study? Why is today's lesson important for your students? How are you starting with the concrete and moving to the abstract?*

TIP 2

Strategies, Resources, and Technologies That Enhance Learning

Good teaching involves much more than randomly placing wonderful resources, technologies, and strategies in front of students with the hope of generating amazing, spontaneous results. Rather, good teaching entails seamlessly coupling numerous intentional actions together. TIP 1 addressed how the "bricks and mortar" of the curriculum structure provides the essential framework to support effective teaching and learning. TIP 2, the focus of this chapter, considers two instructional issues that provide texture to the subsequent learning. Specifically, what are the strategies and resources, including technologies, used to guide instructional practice?

It may seem that strategies and technologies are unrelated concepts—one being the instructional approach taken and the other being an instructional tool used to promote learning. But intentional teaching requires that these two educational components work fluidly together instead of separately. It is futile to bring technologies and other resources into the classroom without thinking carefully about how they will meld with the strategies to be used. When united, strategies and technologies can greatly enhance learning experiences by enhancing intentionality. When teaching lacks intentionality, then learning lacks purpose and clear direction, diverges from the goal and objectives, and appears to be busywork on a given topic. However, when clear intentionality exists, learning includes a focus that unites the curricular framework with the learning strategies and resources so that all students consistently demonstrate solid growth.

TIP 2 focuses primarily on two questions: (1) How well do your selected strategies engage all learners (*Student-Centered Strategies*), and (2) How do the resources and technologies you use provide purpose, enhance engagement, and potentially transform the learning experiences in your classroom (*Resources and Technologies*)?

Student-Centered Strategies

Just as your developmental progress as a teacher differs from that of others because of your prior experiences, content knowledge, and pedagogical skills, each student also differs in his or her starting point and rate of progress. In an effort to counteract students' varying starting points, intense discussions and vast amounts of research have focused on narrowing the achievement gap. If we hope to excel with all students, then learning experiences must provide opportunities to celebrate and encourage students with diverse backgrounds, disparate achievement levels, and different experiences as we interact and grow together as learners.

For years the attempted solution was to tell, model, practice, and then test. In this teacher-centered approach, the teacher tells; the teacher models; the students mimic; and then, on the test, the students reiterate what is essentially still the teacher's knowledge. This approach still prevails in a large percentage of classrooms. So, why the need to change?

First, learners' needs are very different from those of past generations. In today's fast-paced, high-tech society, information is merely a few keystrokes away. Knowing the details of a key historical event, experiencing a Shakespearean play, reciting multiplication tables, or defining Newton's Laws of Motion are all important things, but today's classroom must engage the learner in these experiences, not just require memorization and restatement of facts before moving on. Further, as society has changed in terms of gathering and sharing information, its needs have also changed. Today we must know how to analyze large data sets and communicate solutions to complex problems in domains such as medicine, politics, economics, or engineering. In addition, the demands on the 21st century learner (Partnership for 21st Century Skills, 2013) require that all students demonstrate proficiency in critical thinking, communication (oral and written), collaboration, and creativity. Further,

TIP 2

Strategies, Resources, and Technologies That Enhance Learning

Score	1 (Needs Improvement)	3 (Proficient)	5 (Exemplary)
Student-Centered Strategies (2a)	Facilitates learning through student-centered learning approaches.		
	Strategies and learning are entirely abstract.	Strategies provide concrete experiences and visual means to study abstract concepts and ideas.	Additionally, an explicit link is made to tie the concrete experience with the abstract idea.
	Students are passive learners and instruction focuses mostly on memorization of isolated facts and knowledge.	Students are active learners, engaged during a significant portion of the lesson in ways that support building conceptual understanding.	Students are active learners throughout the lesson and focused on uniting knowledge and skills to promote deep conceptual understanding.
	Learning is only teacher centered and teacher directed.	Instructional strategies are predominantly student centered, requiring more than mimicking or verification of what teacher modeled.	Instructional strategies are solely student centered, requiring more than mimicking or confirmation of what teacher modeled.
Resources and Technologies (2b)	Provides resources and technologies to support learning.		
	Materials and resources don't help make abstract ideas concrete for the learner.	Materials and resources provide concrete and visual means to study abstract ideas.	Materials and resources provide multiple ways for learners to concretely and visually study abstract ideas.
	Materials, resources, strategies, and technologies are largely lacking or lack purpose, distract learning, and lack efficiency.	Materials, resources, strategies, and technologies are not overly distractive and are purposeful and, when possible, are an enhancement to learning.	Materials, resources, and strategies are purposeful, and technologies are transformative (allow us to do something that would not otherwise be possible).

to achieve both the softer skills (e.g., communicating and collaborating) and the core content expressed by the standards, students need to engage deeply with the material. To do so, they need to experience learning in concrete terms that they can relate to before working with abstractions—a point that was also relevant in the discussion on TIP 1.

? *How did you make learning visual and concrete during the last lesson? How will you do so in future lessons? Which came first in your last lesson, the concrete or the abstract?*

Today's instructional strategies need to ensure that students not only develop essential skills (such as the ability to write a clear sentence or fluency with basic multiplication) but also study authentic, complex ideas by working on issues that are meaningful to them (such as creating a persuasive essay surrounding a real cause, calculating the materials needed to build an 1,800-square-foot home, or gathering and communicating scientific evidence to support or refute a solution to a specific problem). This balance means that we no longer tell students everything, ask them to memorize and recite facts back to us, and then move on to more complex topics only as time allows. It means starting with things that are engaging and relevant to students and aligned to the standards and objectives. Attaining the essential skills then becomes purposeful, occurring in parallel with the learning.

I can imagine the objections brewing in the minds of some readers: "Well, how can we explore the complex when Johnny can't read?" "How can Silva begin to interpret a data set when she doesn't know her multiplication tables?" I'll begin by saying that it only makes sense to model learning on how it typically occurs in the real world. Let's consider two prominent contemporary themes that are the epicenters of many conversations around the world: war and climate change. Ideas for how to end war are not likely to emerge by merely asking students to memorize facts related to previous battles or conflicts in the hope that doing so will radically and positively affect future generations. Plausible ideas begin by first exploring broad questions, such as "How can two or more groups feel so strongly that they are willing to go to war over an issue?" and "Is there ever a just cause for war?" Dealing with such questions includes studying the past but also requires that we grab hold of what we know today about people and societies.

Likewise, a full understanding of the complexities associated with climate change requires the ability to solve differential equations and to develop complex models in order to thoroughly map and then project climatic fluctuations. But we can intelligently discuss this topic and others like it before we have all the knowledge or skills necessary for a comprehensive understanding. This is reality. Learning requires that we continue to improve our skills while tackling something meaningful. This approach to learning, with students as active learners, allows us to engage all, challenge all, and differentiate for all.

As such, numerous strategies are available to immerse students in learning rather than keeping them in a robotic, passive state. Specifically, strategies such as inquiry-based instruction, as well as related strategies such as problem- and project-based learning, provide an opportunity for the learner to be deeply and purposefully engaged. For those with little to no experience in facilitating student-centered learning strategies, this is a critical and important area to focus on either individually or as a school. I provide a quick introduction here, but novices in this area should consult additional resources, such as *Succeeding with Inquiry in Science and Math Classrooms* (Marshall, 2013).

Various models have been proposed over the last several decades to guide the facilitation of inquiry-based learning. These include the 5E Model (Bybee et al., 2006), the 4E × 2 Model (Marshall, 2013; Marshall, Horton, & Smart, 2009), and the Learning Cycle (Lindgren & Bleicher, 2005; Marek & Cavallo, 1997). All are predicated on the nonnegotiable idea that students must have the opportunity to explore the concept before the teacher provides a formal explanation. This is perhaps one of the more challenging things for teachers to change, because years of experience and most print curriculums have reinforced the approach of telling first and then confirming, which is analogous to telling the punch line of a joke before delivering the setup. But if we want to engage and motivate students, then we have to create a need for them to question, learn, and create. Students do not come to class wanting to solve quadratic equations, study photosynthesis, or learn the parts of speech. However, when the question is rich enough or the challenge is meaningful enough, we can engage all students in learning the desired content.

? *In your last lesson, how did you actively involve all learners beyond just listening or mimicking? Was the approach effective? If so, what was your evidence? If not, what challenge(s) need to be resolved?*

A five-year research analysis (Marshall & Alston, 2014) has shown that we can narrow the achievement gap while raising the bar of success for all students. Specifically, teachers who were involved in a sustained, two-year professional development experience that focused on improving the quantity and quality of inquiry-based instruction showed promising results: on average, students of participating teachers demonstrated about three to six months' more academic growth when compared with similar students of nonparticipating teachers. This study included over 10,000 students, and comparisons were matched by race, gender, start score, and free-and-reduced-lunch rate.

Although other instructional components are important for complete success with inquiry, a key first step includes switching the paradigm so that students engage in a shared experience on a major concept before the explanation or modeling from the teacher. Some teachers will require considerable time and effort to make this shift, but the reward can be profound. For others, it may be as simple as tweaking the organization of existing lessons so that the "explore" precedes the "explain." To succeed with inquiry, teachers will need to scaffold the learning experiences as students begin to assume more responsibility (TIP 4 provides a detailed discussion on scaffolding and differentiating to ensure greater success for all).

The essence of inquiry is the same for all disciplines, even though the specific issues and characteristics may differ. In a writing class, students can explore what makes a great sentence or paragraph. They can read samples from classical literature, an essay of their own, technical manuals, magazines, songs, novels, or blogs in an effort to understand and then communicate what makes great writing. Once they have identified several examples, they can begin to detail what made the piece stand out. Notice that the students are beginning with something that is concrete and tangible. Then they are ready to discuss and perhaps have the teacher help to clarify why some writing is much better than others, realizing that excellence can and should be qualified by the purpose. For instance, a technical manual's goal is clarity and conciseness, but a novel's goal may be to convey a richly detailed picture of characters through an intricate storyline. The goal then becomes having students improve their writing relative to a specific purpose. Having students memorize specific rules and conventions (abstractions) and then apply them in their writing will most certainly be less effective than having students first read and analyze written works of others, discuss what makes the writing effective or ineffective, and then develop and practice their own writing.

The same approach applies in other disciplines. In science class, students may be exploring the essential question "Can I predict tomorrow's weather?" They could be challenged to see if they can outperform the meteorologists or the weather models. Similarly in economics, students can see if they can beat certain aspects of stock market performance—thus outperforming the professionals. In both examples, real-world, high-challenge contexts engage students while the teacher works with them on learning essential components and concepts in the process. In English language arts or social studies, the teacher might ask students to write a paragraph that conveys a solid argument on a critical current events topic. The learning becomes engaging and student centered because of the topic's relevance, which then allows the teacher to work with students on developing solid arguments by stating claims, articulating evidence (data), constructing counterclaims, rebutting counterarguments, and then developing convincing conclusions. In these examples, the way the lesson is organized and framed creates a need for students to learn the content, which is essential for engaging them in the learning process.

? When are student-centered strategies most valuable for learning in your class? What assistance do you need to excel in your use of these strategies?

Resources and Technologies

It may be that educators lack intentionality in technology more than in any other area. The reasons are many, but the result is a culture that continues to look to technology as the panacea for curing all that ails our modern educational system. In the last 10 years, I have witnessed the same mindset among classroom, school, district, and state leaders: provide it and they will learn. The "it" is more technology.

It seems perfectly logical to desire newer and better technology, resources, and materials for the classroom. However, we typically fail to address many critical questions first. Most common is the lack of meaningful discussion around the question of how the technology will improve students' learning. Closely related is the question of how it will improve instructional effectiveness and management. Also, little has been published, other than anecdotal claims by technology sellers, to suggest that learning, interpersonal interactions, and critical thinking increase with the presence of more technology. Let me provide several examples to make the larger point clear.

? *What technologies and resources do you primarily use that support making learning concrete and visual? What evidence do you have that these resources and technologies are helping learning?*

Example #1: The glorified overhead projector. Over the past decade, districts across the United States have spent thousands to millions of dollars to make sure that an interactive white board is at the front of the classroom. What has changed as a result? Well, most districts have held training sessions with all teachers, but the technology still seems to be used primarily as a glorified overhead projector to show slideshow presentations and take notes. In the process of showing that the school or district has become more high-tech, we typically have done little or nothing to actually improve learning via the white board. In fact, many middle school and high school teachers now complain that they have little to no usable board space for students to share, create, or communicate ideas. So learning may actually be hindered in some cases by focusing on the technology instead of putting the goal of student learning first and then asking how the technology can support or foster it.

To emphasize this point, a recent news story reported that many CEOs, scientists, and leaders in the U.S. Defense Department have given up, at least for now, the use of presentation slides during meetings because these sorts of presentations seem to "act as a straitjacket to discussion." In fact, former U.S. Secretary of Defense Robert Gates said that the CIA has banned slides except for sharing maps and charts (Yu, 2014). This observation is not an indictment of any or all presentation software. If we want learning to be student or learner focused, then we as teachers need to find opportunities to have students talk, collaborate, and create, not to provide flashier sit-and-get presentations. That said, the emphasis should not be on removing all presentation software from the classroom. Rather, we need to consider how we can better use this tool to achieve our goals, including more student engagement.

Example #2: Here it is; now go. Recently there has been an increasing effort to get some form of technology, often in the form of a laptop or tablet, in the hands of every learner. The effort is nice in theory, but what does the implementation look like? For the Los Angeles Unified School District, it was a billion-dollar-plus disaster that was doomed before it started (Dobuzinskis, 2014). In other places, a common scenario includes having the district buy the devices, giving them to the teachers and students just before the school year starts, and then expecting that all the teachers will use them with the students in every class. This approach fails to be intentional in focusing on how to best improve student success. Yes, every K–12 discipline has relevant apps or programs, but which of them actually improve learning, and what is the evidence to support the claim? Did groups of teachers pilot something for roll-out? Did the instructional technology (IT) personnel actually test the infrastructure to know what would happen when 300 or 3,000 students are all on their devices at once? Were curriculum specialists involved to see how the app or program unites with the current learning progressions?

The point is that no technology is inherently good or bad; rather, it is the application of the technological tool that matters. There are examples of interactive white boards, presentation software, and one-to-one programs being used in amazing ways. For instance, Google Earth software or the Google Maps app allows users to take virtual field trips to places not otherwise accessible. Group note taking enables work to be saved and shared with those who are not present, or to be accessed when students need to revisit the work or data. Interactive white boards can provide assessment data and information on class growth via instant-response systems. But we need enhancement and transformative experiences with technology to be the norm, not the exception. Rather than just adding more stuff to the classroom and the teacher's platter, we need to make informed, intentional decisions that are tied to learning and effectiveness.

Although it is true that students have a lot to teach earlier generations about technology, the reverse is also true. Students are frequently more adept at technologies associated with entertainment or social networking sites (e.g., gaming, Instagram, Twitter); but educators can share uses of technology that help to guide learning and knowledge development (e.g., Google Docs or other file-sharing and collaborative technologies). In this sense, technology provides a wonderful synergistic opportunity between students and educators, with both having something powerful to share. When used effectively, technology can motivate and engage learners in ways previously not possible.

? *Which resources and technologies seem to be least effective in your classroom? Which seem to be most effective? Can you replace these limiting technologies, or should they just be eliminated? What evidence supports your intentionality with the technologies you use? What are the* *proposed or existing district technology initiatives or plans, and what is the evidence that they support learning?*

Actions for TIP 2

To guide your discussions, self-reflection, and next steps, consider the following actions that address the central chapter concepts for TIP 2: *Student-Centered Strategies* and *Resources and Technologies.*

Action: Engage the Senses—Make It Concrete

What makes a hero? How can science control a contagious disease? Both of these essential questions may provide some of the impetus necessary to engage learners, but the path to answering these and similar questions must begin by considering them in terms of concrete experiences and representations. *Hero* is an abstract term, and to understand it, students must find concrete examples of people in their lives that model or represent a hero.

Research shows that presenting and investigating ideas in both concrete and abstract terms is far more powerful for learning than doing either in isolation (Pashler et al., 2007). You may need practice to navigate back and forth between a concrete example and an abstract representation, but when you do it successfully, you promote long-term learning and deeply rooted connections. For instance, talking about an apple or writing the word *orange* on the board is an abstract activity. Showing a picture makes the concept less abstract, but actually having an orange or an apple that students can feel, touch, and smell provides a much more concrete experience. Students' writing will likely be much stronger if it is tangible. Observations in science are keener when a first-hand account is possible. Because visual experiences tend to be more powerful than auditory experiences, provide a visual representation (or one as realistic as possible) to assist classroom interactions.

? *What are three ways to increase concrete or authentic experiences for students in the next couple of class periods? What are the most challenging topics for your students to learn? How can you make these topics or concepts more tangible? Do you continue to revisit the concrete representations after moving to the abstract idea? Evidence?*

Action: Get off the Sidelines—Engage Learners

Thinking back through some of your life's experiences, which ones stand out—those in which you watched others or those in which you participated? Which was more memorable and had a greater impact on you: watching a friend run a marathon or running one yourself? Watching a cooking show or cooking a new dish from scratch? Hearing a presentation or developing and delivering a speech of your own? Seeing pictures of a majestic landscape or hiking through the northern Rockies with a friend? There is almost always something to be learned from watching others, but deeper memories come from experiences in which you leave the bleachers and enter the playing field. In the classroom, this means having students work collaboratively to solve complex problems; design and conduct experiments that are more than confirmations of what was presented earlier; or research and then write an essay from the perspective of a historical figure.

How many times have you heard it said or even said to yourself, "You really don't know something until you teach it"? It is so true. We claim to know many things, but when we teach something, we test the depth of our knowledge. Teaching forces us into an active state of learning. An aspiring football player's ability will be severely limited if all he does is watch or read about football. The player has to actively experience football, and then he is ready to begin developing the essential skills and finer points of the game, which may eventually include analyzing a video of a game. The same is true for a pianist, an author, or an astronaut. In the case of astronauts, they participate in as many simulations as possible, because they generally get only one attempt to succeed with the real thing.

Being able to name something and truly knowing something are vastly different things. In mathematics, we can recite addition facts or multiplication tables, but until we truly understand what addition or multiplication means, we are just reciting facts. Although both facts and conceptual understanding are important, facts alone (which tend to be abstract) are not sufficient for lasting and purposeful learning.

? *How do you get students off the sidelines (passive recipients of knowledge) and into the game (active learners)? What resistance do you see from students, and how can it be overcome? In the next lesson or two, what are three tangible opportunities for students to more actively participate in their own learning?*

Action: Move Beyond "Monkey See, Monkey Do" to Student-Centered Learning

Clearly no one instructional strategy is best in all situations. Intentional teachers seek to match the strategy with the objectives and goals. But if the goal includes engaging or challenging the learner, then student-centered strategies are a necessity. Inquiry-based instruction facilitated by the teacher provides an excellent balance between providing students with deeply engaging learning experiences and keeping the learning focused on a central theme or conceptual idea.

For instance, you could have students write their own choose-your-own-adventure story with multiple endings. You could provide graphic organizers to help them organize their ideas and thoughts, and you could facilitate small-group or whole-group interactions based on needs and visible weaknesses you notice during the story-development phase. You could amend the project to integrate the focus and plot around key historical events or scientific discoveries. Notice that the goal is not to just deliver a lecture on how to write a story; rather, students explore, question, and work to develop their thoughts and ideas, with you providing support as students show a need.

In mathematics, guided-inquiry experiences are often shorter lessons focusing on a problem or theme. So if the goal is to understand measures of central tendency, then you could present the following problem: *Five bicyclists live on the same highway at mile markers 1, 4, 10, 15, and 25. Where should they meet to minimize the total distance traveled for the entire group?*

? *How do your strategies help to engage a variety of students? What strategies do you use that target a limited group of students? How can you modify these strategies to engage more students in learning?*

Action: Is IT It? Improve Effectiveness of Technologies

Although only six letters, the question in the heading reminds us that we must consider the purpose and value of the IT (instructional technology) that is being incorporated in schools and classrooms. Remember that technology provides the tool, and the teacher provides the strategy that incorporates the tool. The mindset of simply accumulating more technology needs to be replaced by a more purposeful use of technology.

Moore's Law demonstrates that the processing speeds of computers have continued to increase at a near exponential rate (with the number of transistors used to power the computer doubling about every two years). This growth has moved us from the pixelated, simplistic graphics of early computer games such as the *Oregon Trail* to newer, more complex multiuser interfaces with impressive high-resolution graphics. The growth, however, also puts school leaders in a quandary as to where limited funds for technology, both hardware and software, should be spent, given how quickly apps, programs, and equipment become outdated.

All technology meetings for faculty and school leaders need to be grounded in two underlying principles, which can be expressed as questions. First, how will this technology, specifically, improve learning for students? (Consideration of this question should include identifying what the technology is replacing.) Second, how will this technology improve teacher effectiveness? Grand and generic responses should be warning signs. Specifically, blanket statements such as "This will help students be more successful" or "Teachers will be more effective" are nice, but what do they really mean for a 2nd grade student or a 7th grade social studies teacher? Perhaps a better approach would be to take specific software that is going to be used in class and discuss the pros and cons of using such a program. For instance, if a game is selected for students to use to study math or history concepts, how much time will be spent on peripheral activities (e.g., setting up an avatar, learning the rules, navigating the site), and how much will be focused on the learning goals (e.g., improving computational fluency, studying a historical event)?

? *Because even the newest technology will be quickly outdated, where should you spend limited funds? How will the technology help to improve learning for all? Which tools provide the most benefit to the learner, and why? How do the technologies you use support the need for experiences that are more concrete? Are there ways to make experiences more concrete with and without technology?*

Action: Ensure Purposeful, Transformative Technologies— Not Flash and Glitz

In 2010 Dr. Ruben Puentedura developed the SAMR Model, which defines various levels of technology integration. From least integrated to most integrated, SAMR stands for Substitution, Augmentation, Modification, and Redefinition. Research continues to show that although each level has a positive effect on learning, the larger effects tend to be on the upper (more integrated) end of the model (e.g., modification or redefinition). In a math class, a more advanced and integrated use of technology would include moving from drill-and-practice apps (substitution) to more adaptive apps that base the next problem on how the student answered the previous problem (augmentation). In earth science, this could mean moving from interactive apps (augmentation) to a narrated animation project (modification). The difference between the two lower SAMR levels of substitution and augmentation is that augmentation provides a functional improvement. When studying birds, for instance, a substitution website provides images of birds, whereas an augmentation site includes descriptive information, images, data, and sounds for each bird.

It may already be apparent that the SAMR Model aligns well with Bloom's taxonomy. Although the two are not a perfect match, as we move to higher levels of integration in both, we also challenge students to higher-order thinking. For instance, at the lowest level, substitution, most apps, programs, and technology focus on recall or basic visualization of an idea. At the highest level of redefinition, students are interacting and creating in ways not previously possible without the technology. In some specific examples, substitution technologies (e.g., performing a Google search or using Word, Quizlet, CourseNotes) help to develop skills and knowledge by encouraging learning at the level of remembering and understanding. Augmentation technologies (e.g., Google Docs, PowerPoint, QuickVoice, Explain Everything) allow students to apply what they know through movie making, making a diary, drawing a diagram, or taking a photograph. Modification and redefinition technologies (e.g., Nearpod, WordPress, GarageBand, Edmodo, iMovie, Google+) seek to challenge students to evaluate and create by storytelling, critiquing, videocasting, and animating. The apps mentioned are to illustrate the various levels and should not be seen as absolutes; the level of integration is based on *how the technology is used*. For instance, presentation software can be used as a lower-level means to share notes with students for later recall, but students can also use slides as an interactive presentation-development tool, which illustrates a much higher level of thinking.

Your goal should be to challenge students to engage deeply in the content through the use of technology. To achieve this goal, always be mindful of what the students are achieving with the technology. In some cases, the technology can be flashy and the content is absent or superficial. In such cases, it hinders learning, even though students may be having fun. If your aim is to have students demonstrate deep conceptual understanding by creating something using technology, then make sure that, whenever possible, they use the technology to exceed what they previously could do without it.

? *List all the current technologies that your students are using. What is your goal for the use of these technologies? Is it possible to replace one or more of these technologies so that your students achieve higher-level thinking? Is there a technology that can be added to your class to deepen understanding of a challenging concept?*

TIP 3

Safe, Respectful, Well-Organized Learning Environment

Strolling down the corridor of any school, observers will see a wide range of behaviors and interactions as they walk by each classroom. Some classes are energetic and filled with excitement, while others are dull and stoic; some are filled with challenge and curiosity, while others are characterized by rote activities and busywork. The difference, it appears, centers around the individual teacher's facilitation of management, relationships, and interactions, not the content or curriculum; after all, the content in 8th grade language arts classes is probably the same across classrooms, and school and district initiatives are likely standardized. Yet some teachers make studying Shakespeare a thrilling experience, whereas others provide something analogous to a root canal procedure. As we explore facilitating a safe, respectful, and well-organized environment, let's first consider the juxtaposition of poorly versus effectively managed learning environments.

Here are some warning signs of a poorly managed classroom: (1) the majority of the time before the start of class or during the first 10 minutes is spent addressing questions like "what are we going to be doing today," "what did I miss yesterday," and "what should we do with our homework"; (2) a significant portion of class time is spent on getting students focused, working through procedures, and attending to nonlearning tasks; and (3) both teacher and students are slow to transition from one segment of the lesson to another, and instructional time is largely spent on explaining what the teacher wants from the students.

In contrast, here are some signs of a well-managed classroom: (1) students come in and quickly engage in the goals or assignment posted on the board; (2) students know what is expected and know the procedures, so time is maximized with little to no confusion; and (3) the class has a positive flow, transitions smoothly from one segment of the lesson to another, and is full of energy because students act with clear purpose, know what to do, and quickly get to work.

Most classes fall somewhere between these two descriptions. Where do your classes fall on the continuum? A typical class in middle and high school begins with the teacher actively multitasking (handing back papers, checking in with students, taking attendance, setting up for the class) while the students show a mixed level of engagement as they plod through a warm-up or bell-ringer activity. Analyzing this scene suggests a purposeful plan (typically mandated by schools) that requires students to complete a review question while the teacher handles non-instructional activities. The plan seems solid at first glance because the students are busy while the teacher works through necessary tasks. Although a management rationale might underlie all of this, on closer examination we realize that a huge opportunity to engage the learner has been missed.

Teachers' success (or lack thereof) is highly dependent on their strength in classroom management. If classroom management is compared to a tabletop, then successful management is analogous to a horizontal table that allows things to stay on top of it. More specifically, a flat, horizontal tabletop allows everything placed upon it (instruction, assessments, interactions) to remain stable. As the tabletop tilts and nears vertical, everything eventually falls from its surface—nothing can be achieved. So although effective classroom management is a necessary and vital part of any successful classroom, its primary role is to provide the platform for everything else to occur—the instruction, the strategies, and the interactions.

For many teachers, classroom management is about student behavior, rules, and procedures, which suggests that much of learning is about compliance and conformity. Starting with this belief automatically limits what can be achieved in the classroom. I encourage you to think about management in terms of flow and interactions. Instead of compliance and conformity, the 21st century classroom must be filled with inspiration, challenge, creativity, questions, and interactions. The teacher's role is to guide the interactions in safe, respectful, and collaborative ways while moving instruction forward with a fluidity that maximizes time spent on learning and minimizes noninstructional routines, procedures, and transitions.

TIP 3 focuses primarily on two questions: (1) How do you improve the flow of learning in your classroom (*Classroom Flow*), and (2) How can interactions in your classroom be improved through better classroom management (*Classroom Interactions*)?

Classroom Flow

We all like to feel that our time is valued. Just consider the frustrated faces of drivers sitting in a traffic jam, your annoyance when you're placed on hold during a phone call, or the outbursts of passengers whose flights are delayed or cancelled. School is no exception. Teachers wonder why students go from being excited during lunch to being lethargic and disengaged during class. The reasons are many, but one issue central to the discussion involves how we use and structure classroom time. The pacing, procedures, and routines all provide the framework that allows classroom activity to flow smoothly.

? *What do you need to change to produce a smoother-running, better-managed, more engaging learning environment?*

Some classes seem to just "happen"; that is, they are filled with activities, things, and discussions that may or may not tie to a specific standard or objective. My focus in this book is on being more intentional, so that things happen for a purpose. I liken teaching a great lesson to composing an excellent essay. Essays have many purposes (creative, persuasive, expository), but in all cases, solid writing quickly grabs the reader's attention with a quote, a compelling introduction, or a question to help frame the thesis or premise. Then the writer draws in the reader with illustrative comments, examples, data, or imagery to strengthen and support the thesis. Finally, the conclusion brings all the pieces together by summarizing the key thoughts. This is a gross oversimplification of the essay-writing process, but the point is that there are generally three parts (introduction, body, conclusion) that work together cohesively.

Let's take these general components and see how they apply to a lesson. The introduction for most classes begins with a warm-up or bell-ringer activity that may or may not tie to the lesson. The lack of a

TIP 3

Safe, Respectful, Well-Organized Learning Environment

Score	1 (Needs Improvement)	3 (Proficient)	5 (Exemplary)
Classroom Flow (3a)	Manages instructional time and noninstructional routines smoothly and effectively.		
	Teacher has difficulty properly pacing and refocusing class after transitions; lots of non-learning time is wasted.	Pacing and transitions are efficient, smooth, with little time lost during transitions.	Additionally, students typically respond with automaticity to cues during lesson.
	Instructional procedures are disjointed and lack organization. Interruptions and noninstructional tasks significantly consume time.	Instructional procedures are clear, purposeful, and engaging. Any noninstructional interruptions are brief, with students quickly refocusing.	High automaticity in procedures is evident. After interruptions students quickly return to established routines with little to no prompting from teacher.
	Students behave as if unaware or confused regarding basic routines.	Routines flow smoothly, are known by students, and provide little disruption to learning.	Additionally, students are familiar with and respond promptly to routine cues. Classroom appears to "run itself."
Classroom Interactions (3b)	Manages student behavior effectively; cultivates a respectful and collaborative climate.		
	Behavior management is lacking or poorly implemented. Student behavior significantly compromises classroom safety and instructional progression.	Behavior management is evident, clearly proactive, and appropriately reactive when necessary.	Additionally, students respond promptly to management expectations—consistently refocusing self and others.
	Teacher displays negative affect and lacks patience.	Teacher conveys solid presence, positive affect, and patience.	Additionally, all students are engaged in creating a positive, respectful environment.
	Teacher appears unapproachable, provides little to no support, is condescending, frequently sarcastic, and/or clearly disrespectful.	Teacher is approachable, supportive, and respectful during interactions.	Teacher demonstrates active support for all learners, and students engage in respectful dialogue with peers.

tie could be analogous to beginning an essay with the concluding statement from a previously written piece, in which case a lack of coherence quickly becomes evident. An entire section that follows in the Action Steps (*Ring the Bell Differently to Create Positive Habits and Routines*) is devoted to different approaches to beginning class. I will not discuss the body of the lesson here because it is covered in other TIPs, but I do want to address conclusions. The vast majority of the hundreds of lessons I have seen lack a conclusion or debriefing. Ending a lesson by letting students complete individual work or giving them "free time" misses an extraordinary opportunity to pull the pieces of knowledge together. Students need to see value throughout the lesson, and the opportunities to improve learning dramatically increase when the beginning, middle, and end all build cohesively around a central concept or idea. One suggestion, with more to follow in the action steps later in this chapter, is to use the last five minutes of the class to bring students together for sense-making, reviewing, debriefing, extending their thinking, or to leave them thinking about a question that you will start class with tomorrow.

? *How do you begin and end class? Why do you do it this way, and is it the best means to manage and engage students?*

In addition to coherent lessons, another aspect of classroom flow consists of norms and routines. Incorporating norms and routines into instruction is beneficial for multiple reasons. All students, but particularly many with special needs, perform better when they have norms and routines to guide them. Routines involve everything from how students enter the classroom and begin class to what they should do with their homework. These are physical elements, but routines and norms also involve interpersonal aspects, such as raising hands to talk or expectations for how to effectively respond to others during discussions. In classes where students work with materials that could be a safety concern, such as science classes, routines are especially important to maximize classroom flow and to ensure student safety.

Early in the school year, it is important to devote considerable emphasis and time, along with frequent reminders, to ensuring that routines and norms become habitual. Once that happens, then occasional reminders are enough to keep the classroom operating consistently. If routines and norms are inconsistent, particularly early in the year, then the desired habits rarely form.

Finally, make sure your routines logically follow from your instructional sequence. For example, if you typically review homework at the beginning of class, training students to put their homework in a folder as they enter the room is self-defeating. Instead, your routine should call for students to have homework out on their desk with their correction pen ready (something different from what they used for the written portions of the homework) before the tardy bell rings. You can allot two or three minutes to discuss the homework to see where students struggled most, and then post answers or take some time to address the issues that posed the most difficulty. Why spend time going through material that students understood? Doing so wastes everyone's time.

? *What are the most common routines and procedures you use in your classroom? Are they safe, efficient, and minimally disruptive?*

Classroom Interactions

When someone says "classroom management," teachers frequently think of behavior management. If, however, the classroom is well managed and arranged, then behavior management becomes a small background component of your classroom interactions. Undoubtedly some students are extremely challenging to work with—often for a variety of reasons—but it is important to note that students are frequently problematic in only some of their classes. Why do some students behave well and even engage in learning in some classes while being disruptive in others? This situation largely stems from the management practices and relationships that have been established in one class over another. The goal is to make productive behavior consistent.

? *What is expected behavior in your class, and do your students consistently meet these expectations? How can you increase the proactive nature of behavior management in your class?*

Although behavior management is essential to achieving maximal success with students, other important elements of classroom management include the teacher's "presence" and the respect shown in human interactions. If a teacher fails to gain student attention, then respect and management efforts quickly unravel.

In many ways, we are like salespeople in our classrooms, but our salesmanship typically differs from that of a car salesman or a clerk at the mall. Specifically, our presence is built upon how effectively we can sell our goods (knowledge, skills, content) and our services (respect, collaboration, interaction). Many teachers can convey the importance of the goods, but the greatest challenge—and perhaps what sets excellent teaching apart from ordinary teaching—is the degree to which students engage in the services, deeply interacting with the content or respectfully disagreeing with ideas (not people). To sell students on the services requires solid presence, positive affect, and tremendous patience.

If we anger easily, are consistently curt with students, or commonly display a negative attitude, we end up dividing students into two groups: those who rapidly achieve mastery and are resilient (the successful) versus those who struggle at times or may be less confident (the unsuccessful). This setup suggests a fixed mindset around those who will achieve and those who will not. The point is not that we all have to be warm, fuzzy, and coddling, but we do need to be confident in our presence without being cocky or demeaning to any student. Many times our actions are subtle and can be adjusted when someone calls attention to the issue. For instance, I can quickly determine if a teacher is going into an honors or an AP class versus a general or lower-level class by the body language shown or the first few words uttered as the tardy bell rings.

? *How would others describe your classroom presence? What can you do to improve your presence?*

Finally, a well-managed class is highly dependent upon respect—respect given by the teacher to students, by students to the teacher, and among students as they interact with each other. It is nearly impossible to achieve meaningful discussions in a classroom without students and teachers having respect. It is important to be aware that not all students (or adults) give respect from the onset. For many students, respect is something that must be earned rather than given upfront. This is not something that should be taken personally. It may be a result of a cultural difference, a learned behavior outside of school, or a defense mechanism. If students do not show respect from the onset, it is important not to overreact. Instead, be consistent—and persistent—in your expectations, so that respect becomes the norm in your classroom. TIP 5 discusses how to facilitate effective classroom interactions. For our current discussion, let's compare respectful versus disrespectful environments.

In respectful classrooms, teachers are approachable and supportive and seek to build confidence and self-esteem among their students.

In a disrespectful environment, teachers convey condescension, sarcasm, and lack of support. We can be firm in demeanor, but never mean. Personal attacks (even subtle ones) or sarcastic comments that ultimately demean students with humor are never helpful in efforts to encourage positive classroom environments where students are willing to take risks.

? *How does "respectful, supportive, and approachable" look in your class? What needs to change to improve your classroom environment?*

Actions for TIP 3

To guide your discussions, self-reflection, and next steps, consider the following actions that address the central chapter concepts for TIP 3: *Classroom Flow* and *Classroom Interactions*.

Action: Maximize Instructional Flow

Time is a precious commodity to teachers. Most middle and high school teachers spend 180 hours (1 hour per day for 180 days) or less with students and are challenged to help their students excel during that time. Elementary teachers typically have more time with students but must help them achieve success in multiple disciplines. In either case, effective use of time is a critical issue.

Teachers often say that they could do much better with their students if they had more time. I like to flip this thinking and ask, How could you do better if you had less time? Asking yourself what you would do if you had even less time forces you to focus on what is truly important.

Having been in hundreds of classrooms over the past dozen years (teaching, observing, coteaching), I found that the average teacher spends about 20 percent of class time on noninstructional matters. The percentage goes much higher when it includes the amount of time allotted for individual work to be completed with little or no support. The point is that we need to be good stewards of our time. It may be acceptable to waste an hour of our own time, but wasting an hour of class time is the equivalent of approximately 30 wasted person-hours (1 hour for each student in class).

One way to begin thinking more intentionally about your time is to break down how the time was apportioned over several days. Then put the specific categories (warm-up, notes, handing out papers) into broader categories such as instructional versus noninstructional time;

collaborative work and relationship building versus individual work; or time students spent engaged versus time spent passively receiving knowledge.

? *What is your most ineffective use of time ("ineffective" being time spent in ways that do not help move students toward achieving broader goals)? How can you tweak your instructional flow to engage more students for longer periods of time?*

Action: Use Efficient Procedures to Gain Effective Learning

An effectively engaged classroom frequently requires multiple transitions during any given class period. If a 50-minute class has four major transitions, then students need to be adept at smooth, quick transitions to refocus. A 15-second transition four times per class equals a minute of class every day, but a 90-second transition four times per class consumes 6 minutes of class every day. Over the course of one week, this is the difference between 5 minutes and 30 minutes. Whether it relates to transitioning or following commonly used instructional procedures, efficiency is critical.

Emphasize *efficiency* for routines and procedures, but emphasize *effectiveness* for learning. When taking attendance, handing out papers, collecting student work, or engaging in any other noninstructional routine, the emphasis must be on improving efficiency. Learning is a totally different game, and it is important not to push efficiency at the expense of effectiveness. Ultimately, the goal is getting students to achieve at the highest level possible. So if you are dealing with noninstructional issues, then your focus needs to be on minimizing time and energy—thus promoting efficiency. If, however, you are dealing with instructional issues such as facilitating collaborations, guiding peer editing, or designing an experiment, then your focus must be primarily on effectiveness. Any minutes gained being efficient with noninstructional behaviors can free up considerable time for instructional and relational experiences. Further, increasing efficiency in noninstructional matters is an effective deterrent for behavior problems. A teacher whom I have worked with for several years asked if I could come in and teach one of the toughest classes that she had encountered in 25 years of teaching. Although everything wasn't solved in one class period, her comment after the class was, "Wow, you didn't stop! Students were given time to work when appropriate, but there were no breaks between things."

Some people's mantra is, Why do today what can be put off until tomorrow? For those who thrive under pressure, this behavioral pattern may lead to some success, but procrastinating in establishing classroom routines and procedures usually means the habits never form or form too late in the year to save much time. If you believe, as you should, that spending time on learning and relationships is critical, then build routines and procedures early on so that time can be maximized for other more important things. Time invested early in the year can be reaped all year long.

? *How can I improve transition in my classroom? What other frequent procedures can I make more efficient in my class? What are the key routines in my classroom? How do I ensure that all these routines become everyone's habits?*

Action: Ring the Bell Differently to Create Positive Habits and Routines

What student comes to class excited to engage in a 3- to 10-minute bell-ringer activity that reviews a question from yesterday or that mimics a question similar to what will appear on a standardized test later in the year? The point is not whether students need to review, reflect, or write; rather, the point is when and how should that occur?

Let me suggest another approach. Begin by engaging all learners in something substantive and important to them. The question can be provocative, it can probe a curiosity, or it can be asked by the students. The point is to get them thinking, exploring, and talking from the very beginning.

Think about the last time you went to a movie. The theater owners didn't start by showing you the most boring parts of the feature movie. Instead, they showed you the coming attractions—the most exciting or engaging clips they could find to get you to invest in coming back soon. How about trying something similar for your class? Provide some highlights of the coming attractions for the days or weeks ahead. This might be a great idea for Mondays, when students often have difficulty reengaging in school after two or more days off.

Other examples include finding current events that students are excited or curious about, relating the upcoming lesson to the students in some personal way, or imparting a bit of humor. Humor can lighten the mood and encourage students to take a risk even though some of the work for the day might be extremely challenging. Please note that there are many kinds of humor. Sarcasm is an example of an unacceptable form that makes a student the target of the laugh, but puns, riddles, or jokes that get students thinking about the content can be fun and contagious—and many students will begin adding their own humor to the mix.

How you start class is important, but so is how you end class. Most classes just stop—here is your assignment, be prepared for a quiz tomorrow, finish your lab report. Instead, how about taking time to debrief and pull the pieces together? You can put the last few minutes to good use by using them to clarify areas of confusion or to review or practice concepts that have been learned today or in previous days. Spending time this way also allows an additional opportunity to show how the learning connects to the students, to the discipline, and to other disciplines.

? *What things frustrate you most in your classroom? Is there a routine or procedure that, if it became a habit, could eliminate or at least reduce this frustration? What do you need to do to make this routine or procedure become a habit with your students? What are three or four approaches that you can take to more effectively begin and end class?*

Action: Be Proactive

Being proactive in classroom management is essential for a smoothly running class, and this is the area where you may struggle, particularly if you are a relatively new teacher. Behavior management, a significant component of classroom management, succeeds when you command a solid presence, institute fair rules with appropriate consequences, are consistent in following those rules, and show respect for all.

Many books have been written on classroom management. Examples include *The First Days of School* (Wong & Wong, 1998), *Teaching with Love and Logic* (Fay & Funk, 1998), *Discipline with Dignity* (Curwin, 2008), and *Classroom Management That Works* (Marzano, 2003). But you need to personalize whatever recommendations and guidelines you choose to follow. Regardless of the plan adopted, you will probably find that the greatest challenge is to be consistent.

As classrooms become more student centered, you, the teacher, need to be in better control. Proficient control requires that you model the actions that you expect students to perform, such as aptly and efficiently transitioning from one task to another. For some, this means learning to accept a certain amount of noise in the classroom. Effective teachers quickly learn when noise is expected, what levels are acceptable, what "productive noise" sounds like, and how to assist those who are easily distracted by noise.

? *Where are you consistent or inconsistent with enforcing your rules? In areas where you are inconsistent, decide if the rule is needed in the first place or if something needs to be changed. How can you become more proactive at the beginning of the year to avoid issues later on?*

Action: Build Your Presence as a Teacher

Each semester, I ask my student teachers to tell me what their reputation will be from their students' perspective. After a moment of puzzled stares, they quickly realize that they play an active role in helping to shape a positive, desirable reputation for themselves. We often do not know how others perceive us, so it is important to find a venue that allows objectivity in gauging our affect and the level of respect given to and modeled for others.

Here are some ways to measure the classroom climate that you help facilitate: (1) shoot a video of yourself teaching a lesson and then review it, looking for key aspects; (2) ask the opinion of a colleague or friend who is able to observe you teach and is willing to be totally honest with you; (3) give a brief survey to your students with the promise of anonymity.

? *What is your reputation among your peers and among your students? Is it what you desire? If not, what steps can you take to personally begin shifting the current perception to your desired perception?*

TIP 4

Challenging, Rigorous Learning Experiences

Although many people decry apathy's prevalence in the classroom, most teachers feel limited in their ability to confront and eradicate this menace to learning. Apathy manifests in many ways but is often indicated when students disengage, appear overwhelmed, or act angry. Regardless of the archetypal face that it assumes in the classroom, the results are students who largely underperform.

Csikszentmihalyi (1997) suggests that perhaps our expectations (in terms of both skill and level of challenge) are too low when students display apathy. The natural inclination when a student does not know an answer or shows that a fundamental skill is missing is to progressively reduce the difficulty of the questions or assignments until the student answers correctly—often culminating in a ridiculous hunt-and-seek game of simply finding the answer in the text and filling in the missing word on the worksheet. I suggest this approach is the opposite of what it should be. When students have bought in to the assignment, the topic, or the class, they will put forth tremendous effort to achieve success. In some cases, they exert this effort so they won't let you down. More important, as their confidence starts to improve, they increase their performance because they don't want to let *themselves* down.

The newer standards provide a good opportunity to raise expectations for all. As I noted earlier, it is no longer sufficient for students to merely list and describe facts, names, or dates. With the newer standards, teachers must facilitate learning that requires students to demonstrate ideas, provide evidence, model complex concepts, and design experiments. Clearly the task of creating more challenging and rigorous learning opportunities is not as simple as just raising expectations. If it were that simple, then student achievement would be soaring.

We face a bit of a conundrum. We live in a world that perpetuates the idea that if we are good at something it will be easy; but we also know that the greatest satisfaction comes when we stretch ourselves physically or intellectually to achieve the greatest possible outcome. Before students willingly put forth their best work, they must see inherent value in the risk that they are about to take. This chapter begins to unravel the complexities associated with creating a culture of high expectations and challenge while discussing what instruction that challenges all students looks like.

TIP 4 essentially focuses on two questions: (1) How do you establish a climate of high expectations and a willingness to persevere in the face of challenge (*Culture of Challenge*), and (2) How do the learning experiences you provide appropriately challenge the learner (*Instructional Challenge*)?

Culture of Challenge

The act of setting clear, high expectations will not in itself eradicate apathy and instantly generate an inviting culture of challenge, but it is one of the first, crucial steps in allowing those outcomes to occur. Think for a moment about opposing ends of the spectrum. In one class, students arrive and basically just survive the 180-day experience that we call 3rd grade, 7th grade math, U.S. history, or physics. The teacher presents and the students follow and mimic what was modeled—filling in blanks, taking quizzes and tests with no apparent direction or expectation except for the successful completion of the worksheet or assessment. At the other end of the continuum is a classroom where students push themselves, challenge each other, and expect only the best from their teacher.

Few teachers will admit to just going through the motions with their students, as conveyed by the first scenario, but hundreds of classroom observations across the nation have shown me that relatively few can honestly say that they have a created the second scenario—a culture in which the teacher and students collectively and consistently pursue high expectations each day. The question then becomes, How do you, and potentially your teacher colleagues, begin to move the level of expectation from little or none to clear, consistent, and challenging expectations for all students—and teachers?

Excellence in teaching is evident when students begin achieving things beyond what they would achieve with their own abilities. Specifically, excellence in teaching provides the motivation, guidance, and encouragement to students to achieve something that they previously thought was impossible.

? *What do high expectations look like in your classroom, and how do you know you have set the expectations appropriately high? Would others agree that your expectations are high enough? Evidence?*

TIP 4

Challenging, Rigorous Learning Experiences

Score	1 (Needs Improvement)	3 (Proficient)	5 (Exemplary)
Culture of Challenge (4a)	Facilitates climate of perseverance and high expectations.		
	Expectations are set low and/or not communicated clearly to students.	Teacher sets and communicates appropriate, high expectations.	Teacher and students collectively pursue high expectations.
	Persistence, perseverance, and self-monitoring are not modeled by teacher or demonstrated by students.	Persistence, perseverance, and/or self-monitoring are modeled by teacher and demonstrated by most students.	Persistence, perseverance, and/or self-monitoring are demonstrated by all students, regardless of ability level.
Instructional Challenge (4b)	Provides challenging, differentiated learning experiences.		
	Lesson is superficial, lacking challenge or rigor.	Lesson provides appropriate challenge.	Lesson provides significant opportunities where all students are appropriately challenged.
	Instruction is uniform in delivery and lacks scaffolding to make learning accessible to most.	Instruction is differentiated and provides appropriate scaffolds to address varied levels of readiness.	Learning is differentiated to challenge all learners, with appropriate scaffolds used to maximize learning.

We have all seen it and perhaps experienced it ourselves—that unrelenting desire to keep doing something again and again until we have achieved mastery, victory, or the satisfaction that we crave. I have seen this happen when kids refuse to put down a new digital device or game; I have seen this with adolescents who want to master a move on the basketball court or on the soccer field; and I have seen this with students when they become so intrigued with a question or problem that they don't want to stop until they have solved it. Perseverance is a hunger or excitement that burns from within the student or teacher. Although it is unlikely that students will come to your classroom with an intrinsic need to study and understand all the concepts or standards that you seek to address in a given year, it is vital that you find approximately five to eight things about your discipline that you can use to anchor your push for excellence.

Students quickly learn that if they wait long enough, the teacher or other students will provide the answer to whatever problem needs to be solved. When they become accustomed to looking to others for the answer and to giving up before solving challenging problems, then we achieve the opposite of perseverance.

Perhaps one of the best ways to improve persistence and perseverance in your class is to begin with yourself. If your passion is reading or the arts, you may have little persistence when it comes to math or science. Ask yourself if there are areas in which you tend to persist and other areas in which you tend to become frustrated and quit. Most likely the latter areas are those in which you have little interest or do not feel confident in your ability. If you don't model perseverance for your students in your classroom, your students will tend to persist only in areas where they naturally feel confident, knowledgeable, or talented.

I discuss scaffolding and readiness in more detail later in this chapter, but it's worth mentioning that one way to help students begin to become more persistent learners is for you and your students to each set goals that you will hold each other accountable for during the semester. Guided self-monitoring will allow you and your students to chart your progress and your growth. For students, the first goal may be to persist in working on math problems for at least a minute before asking for help (most students persist for seconds in math, not minutes). If your personal goal is to learn more effective strategies to teach students or to complete your master's degree, then set targets and share your growth with your students. For instance, what did you learn through your research that makes you a better teacher, and where did you persist? Find multiple examples of students and adults who persisted in an effort to illustrate for your students that perseverance and continued commitment to goals lead to success. Use examples of individuals who have persevered through obstacles and challenges (e.g., Vincent Van Gogh, the Beatles, Michael Jordan, Albert Einstein, Babe Ruth, Dr. Seuss, Abraham Lincoln).

? *In what ways can you encourage persistence, perseverance, and self-monitoring?*

Instructional Challenge

Failure is easy. It is easy to come to class and not do your work; it is easy to not do the homework; it is easy to sign your name and turn in a blank quiz or test. In far too many classrooms, we have made failure the easy route to take.

My goal is to make failure extraordinarily difficult for a student through my persistence, support, and unwavering belief in my students' success—not by dumbing down the material. I partially understand comments from teachers who say, "My students need to assume responsibility—my job is to teach and theirs is to learn." I very much want my students to assume responsibility; but the challenge that I put before them needs to be developmentally, intellectually, and emotionally appropriate for them.

Let's back up for a moment. If you teach 5th grade and a student comes to your class with a record of failure and many missing skills, do you really think just encouraging her to take responsibility for her own work because it is what is expected in middle school will make her suddenly start working to expectations? Many have come to embrace the famous *Apollo 13* mantra, "Failure is not an option" (Howard, 1995). The scene in the movie is a powerful metaphor for what successful classrooms look like, but our actions need to align with our words. I let my students know that ultimately they are in control of whether they succeed or fail—I can't force a student to complete a test, an assignment, or homework. However, I also let them know that I will do everything in my power to provide a classroom where they can succeed. Further, I make it a miserable experience—not easy—for a student to fail. I challenge students to give their best every day. I find them at lunch; I return a paper and ask them to resubmit it when I know it is not their best; I provide review or help sessions at times that are convenient for students; I call them at home; I send them e-mail messages; I involve parents in supportive, not punitive, ways. Yes, students need to do the work; but for students who have experienced years of failure, it is imperative to provide enough support for them to achieve success. Once a student consistently displays success, it will be time to encourage him to begin assuming individual responsibility.

? *What should be the minimum level of work that you will accept from all students? How do you encourage students to exceed the expectations that you set? What is the level of challenge in your most recent lesson, and is it sufficient?*

Learning in our classrooms will succeed only partially until we realize that we all have different needs. The first reaction to this statement is often acknowledging that, yes, we all have differing needs, but then quickly retorting that there is no possible way to address all those individual needs when teaching 30 or 130 students per day. It doesn't matter if we are talking about young children or career teachers; we all come with differing needs, individual agendas, unique values denoting what is important, and differing areas of strength and of weakness.

My work with teachers has demonstrated the many ways in which we all differ. Some possess a rich and solid content knowledge; others are most adept at building relationships with students and parents; others have greater experience in being creative in their instructional approaches. So when we come together for professional development, it is imperative for me, as a facilitator, to address these different expectations and needs.

The same is true for us when we work with our students in the K–20 classroom. The overarching goal may be the same for all, but how to get there often varies. One thing is certain: the opportunity to differentiate for student needs is greatly limited when we lecture or use direct instruction as our primary instructional strategy. We may see short-term gains, but long-term success for the greatest number of students is limited when our methods lack variety.

Although many books and manuscripts have been written on differentiated instruction (e.g., Tomlinson, 2014; Tomlinson & McTighe, 2003), the core question remains, How can the teacher effectively respond to the varying needs of all learners? Differentiation can be achieved through the curriculum (both content and process), through the assessments or products, and through the climate established in the classroom. Knowing how students learn best, incorporating their interests and affinities, and basing decisions on student readiness are all critical considerations when the goal is to maximize differentiated approaches in the classroom.

How we scaffold our students' learning experiences is important to ensure that the greatest possible depth and rigor are achieved. If we think about learning as climbing stairs, there are times when the stairs are too small or too shallow. This is when students quickly become bored and can easily gain the knowledge and understanding without help from the teacher or others. At other times the stairs are too large or too steep; this is when students are expected to progress faster than they currently can. The goal is to find the zone in which students are challenged to increase their knowledge, performance, or achievement but can do so without becoming overwhelmed in the process. Our goal as teachers is to help increase the complexity, challenge, and level of difficulty that students can tackle with and without our assistance.

? *Where are the best opportunities to differentiate the learning in your current lesson or unit, and how can you best scaffold the learning? How do you maximize learning today, given students' various levels of readiness and ability?*

Actions for TIP 4

To guide your discussions, self-reflection, and next steps, consider the following actions that address the central chapter concepts for TIP 4: *Cultural Challenge* and *Instructional Challenge*.

Action: Remember the "Marshmallow Test" and Build Students' Self-Control

An experiment known as the Marshmallow Test, which began in the 1960s, has shown the importance of self-control and delayed gratification in future social and cognitive success. Originally administered to preschoolers more than 30 years ago, the test is quite simple. Give a child an option: Eat one marshmallow now or wait and be rewarded with two when the researcher returns. This test of self-control and delayed gratification has enormous implications for the K–12 classroom. Longitudinal data based on the original participants in the Marshmallow Test show that those who are able to exhibit self-control perform higher on the SAT, have a lower body mass index, have higher social and cognitive function, and demonstrate an overall greater self-worth even 30 years later (Mischel, 2014; Schlam, Wilson, Shoda, Mischel, & Ayduk, 2013).

Many teachers think of self-control issues in terms of classroom management (getting students to sit in their seats, having students follow instructions, getting students to behave properly). However, self-control and delayed gratification have much larger and far-reaching implications. Specifically, self-control is largely a habit that is developed (or not) and can be reinforced (or not) by the classroom teacher. Self-control is an ally to persistence. Students with little to no self-control respond impulsively to math problems; they write down the first idea that pops into their head for an essay or an answer on a worksheet; and they test hypotheses only once in a science lab. A lack of self-control in the learning process results in a lack of student self-monitoring, which includes checking solutions, revising work, and verifying test results.

You can greatly assist students who may lack persistence by requiring that they show their work on the way to reaching a solution, mark up their copy to indicate edits, or detail multiple test results. Getting this behavior to become a habit will ensure greater achievement and accuracy in student work. This also requires that you ask students to do more than just fill in blanks on a worksheet. Students must see the value of what you ask of them before you can expect them to develop the habit of self-control.

How can you promote self-control and delayed gratification in your class? What needs to change relative to your interactions in the class to promote greater perseverance?

Action: Build Perseverance—but Know When to Toss in the Life Preserver

Resilience is inextricably linked to its cousins, perseverance and effort. Specifically, how we respond to difficulty and challenge determines our fortitude in being able to persevere and continue applying significant effort. As we become more resilient, our resolve strengthens and we willingly take the risk to accept greater challenges, which then require greater perseverance. The curriculum must be student centered and engaging if the goal is to encourage resilience and promote perseverance. When learning is solely teacher centered, the knowledge, the solution path, and the processes used all remain the intellectual property of the teacher and are borrowed by the students only to restate or mimic solutions and answers. Once learning becomes student centered, then students must begin to puzzle their way through unknown questions and curiosities on their way to solutions and further questions. Many educators hold the misconception that struggling students prefer less complicated tasks, yet the research indicates that they actually favor assignments that spark curiosity and encourage thinking (Benard, 2004).

Promoting greater perseverance is not quite as easy as just asking a few really good questions to pique curiosity. To succeed, you must stretch the time students are willing to persevere from seconds or less to minutes or more. This requires you to gauge when to toss students the life preserver and when to let the students or groups tread water a bit before providing support. Remember that the first premise requires that the curriculum be more student centered, so the puzzle or curiosity needs to be more than just a confirmation of what you told them or modeled for them.

As a specific example, when the class is studying genetics, you could begin by having students develop and present a possible model of how traits are passed from one generation to the next. This should ideally be done before a discussion of Punnett squares (a kind of diagram used to predict the outcome of a breeding experiment). The point is not that students will present a perfect model but that they will begin to tackle complex questions using their current skills. Then when they learn about Punnett squares, the concept has value and meaning. In a history class, you could provide students with details leading up to a major conflict (masking details that would allow students to identify the actual event). You could challenge them to propose how they would resolve the situation, and then share the actual historical record, detailing how the event really unfolded. In mathematics, students are often highly reliant on the teacher to know how to solve a problem. Why not provide manipulatives or scenarios and then see if they can solve the problem?

The tendency is to think that students are not able to solve or to begin solving a problem without the teacher first modeling one of the various solution paths. Instead, the approach should involve students working on a problem and, after persevering for a certain amount of time, realizing they need guidance (not the solution) to solve it; or, in some cases, they will discover that they actually are able to generate a solution. Remember that the habit of persistence and perseverance will need to be developed over time; it won't happen on the first attempt.

In English, an example of a teacher-centered approach to writing involves reading a sample of a well-written sentence or paragraph, discussing what made it so, and then requiring students to write their own well-written paragraph that follows the sample. In such cases, the students will mimic the sample. In a more student-centered classroom, teachers can provide a topic and allow students to write the best paragraph that they can (incidentally, this activity serves as an effective pretest). From there, students can peer-edit the work of others or read some examples from authors or from the newspaper or from award-winning student essays. Then they can begin to discover how to reconsider their own work and make it stronger. Thus they begin with their own work and persist until they achieve excellence, instead of taking the teacher-provided examples and parroting them. It is important to realize that regardless of the discipline, students will need practice to increase their competence and accuracy; when the practice follows the self-generated experience, students see a greater purpose in their work.

Make sure that you frequently and explicitly communicate to students why you are expecting them to do more than just watch you and then parrot the information. Remember that a certain amount of mental pain goes along with persistence and effort. Specifically, you are asking students to develop a new mental habit that deviates from the brain's default mode of doing what is easiest. Yet effortful learning changes the brain, so it is important to continue to support and model persistent effort (Brown, Roediger III, & McDaniel, 2014).

? *What are two or three topics or concepts in which you want students to demonstrate great perseverance this semester? In what areas are you persistent as a teacher, and do your students explicitly see you persevering toward excellence? Examples? How can you make persistence a part of your classroom culture?*

Action: Match the Challenge to Current Ability

As a child, I remember experiencing exhilaration one moment and sadness the next when playing the game Chutes and Ladders. In an instant, I could move from near the bottom of the game board to the very top. The opposite was also true; I could be nearing the final square only to land on a chute that would send me cascading toward the bottom.

For many students, learning is very similar; they watch others "get it" quickly while they struggle and seem to get further and further behind.

How we respond to these differences distinguishes us as educators. We must move beyond just allowing the struggling student to repeatedly flounder and fail. By the time students reach middle school and high school and have experienced years of failure, how can we be shocked that they are not excited to begin another "prison" term in school? Likewise, just because students quickly show mastery of the material, we can't leave them alone and expect them to leap to increasingly higher levels of success.

Nor is the answer found in tracking and ability grouping. It frequently pacifies the parents of high-performing kids, but all suffer as a result. Reviewing a little history shows that tracking was and commonly still is used as a tool for separating white, privileged students from the perceived lower-achieving African American students (Mickelson, 2003). These findings date back to federal court cases as early as the 1850s, such as *Roberts v. The City of Boston,* which upheld the notion that separate curriculums were needed for whites and blacks because of the inherent differences in the abilities of the races.

We can't continue to perpetuate these stereotypes. In the real world, we don't track people in the same way. For example, although some teachers currently demonstrate that they are more adept at their craft and spend more time preparing for lessons than others, we don't separate the top teachers from those who are less successful. Why should it be any different for our students? Yes, I can hear the rumblings that this stance might generate, but tracking or ability grouping is a practice that should be stopped. Once we begin to understand the strength that diversity—including diversity in current ability—provides, then we can begin to concentrate on differentiating so that all learners succeed. Realize that separating students into different classes by their perceived ability level is not what is meant by differentiation.

As students work in teams or individually to solve challenges, perplexities, scenarios, or inquiries, you can vary the degree of support that you provide. For ESOL students or students who struggle with basic literacy, you could provide a list of key vocabulary with illustrations and succinct definitions on a laminated card to help guide their conversations, writings, and explorations. They may already have these in their notes (or not), but the goal is to reduce the cognitive load and struggle with things that are secondary to succeeding with the given lesson. In mathematics, you could provide clear examples for students who have been struggling with the concept as they work on computational fluency. For students who pick up the idea or concept quickly, you could provide additional challenges or questions for them to explore. To help students see this work as a challenge rather than punitive, alter the assignment slightly by saying, "Since you clearly have demonstrated that you have achieved mastery with the basic concept, I would like for you to complete problems 6–12 on the problem set instead of 1–8." Other students may want to try those problems as well, which means that you have raised the level of challenge for all. Your overriding goal may be to get all students to be competent in solving problems 6–8, but you can see that some may need scaffolding to get there and others need additional challenges to spur their thinking beyond the minimum. The ability to differentiate and scaffold for individual or group needs applies to all disciplines and all grade levels.

? *At what specific places in your curriculum can you appropriately increase the level of challenge for your students or groups of students? How are you checking to see if students are ready for the challenge or rigor that you place before them? When students show an inability to respond properly to a prompt, an exercise, or a complex problem, what are at least three different ways that you can respond to the situation while still keeping the level of challenge high?*

Action: Rethink Your Finish Line and Take a New Look at Differentiation

For many school districts, the finish line is very clear. It appears on the day when the standardized test or end-of-course exam is given in the spring. To emphasize that this is, indeed, the finish line, many schools and teachers essentially stop teaching once this test has been given. Instruction frequently transitions to babysitting. Class time becomes time to view videos or do things that students might like but that aren't valued.

Although I have an enormous problem with all the time wasted at the end of the school year, my point is really more about how to best prepare students for the finish line. An additional problem is that many preliminary "finish lines" are erected at various times during the year, which can greatly inhibit students' willingness to take risks and submit their best work. When all assignments are punitive (graded solely for right or wrong answers), then students tend to be more cautious by providing only what they think the teacher is looking for.

Because you have students in your classes for an entire semester or a full year, you need to keep reminding them that the goal or final target is the knowledge and abilities they achieve by the end of the year—not who can answer everything correctly today. Yes, there are quizzes and measures along the way, but readiness for each topic or concept being studied varies with each person. If students are learning how to convert fractions to decimals or how to write an expository essay, each of them grows to understand the concepts being studied at a different pace and with differing degrees of depth.

This reality brings up the issue of how you can succeed with all students, given their differing abilities and levels of readiness. First, remember that the goal is not necessarily that everyone achieve mastery today. The finish line is ultimately at the end of the year—or beyond.

The goal then becomes understanding the various levels of readiness of all students and modifying instruction to address these needs. One recommended change is to move away from mostly mass or block practice and toward mixed practice (also known as interleaved practice). Specifically, block practice provides students with only the same types of problems or skills that were modeled, discussed, or experienced that day or that week. In mathematics, it means that if students are studying improper fractions, all problems they receive involve improper fractions. With mixed practice, which emphasizes the current concept as well as others that have been studied, students begin to improve long-term memory and to see the connectedness of their learning. Further, it allows students who may not have achieved mastery on Monday to continue to work with the skill even, say, two weeks later, until they get it. The type of practice used in the classroom is analogous to various diets—mass/ block practice is a binge-and-purge diet, with little retained after the fact. Mixed practice is analogous to eating a balanced diet that includes all the food groups.

Mixed practice seems counterintuitive. If we want to be good at something, it seems that we just need to practice, practice, practice that one thing before moving to another. However, data show that the quick, short-term gains common for mass practice are soon lost (Brown et al., 2014). Learning associated with mixed practice appears slower at first, but as the end of the term (the finish line) approaches, the results demonstrate deeper, more connected, longer-term gains (Brown et al., 2014). Results have shown that interleaved or mixed practice can result in learning gains that are more than 200 percent above classes that use mass practice (Bjork, Dunlosky, & Kornell, 2013; Rohrer & Taylor, 2007). So to get students and parents to support this approach, clear consistent communication is critical—particularly since it is counter to most people's experience.

For example, to become a great soccer player, you don't spend all day practicing shots on goal and then come back tomorrow to work on footwork, followed the next day with a clinic on passing. Although some educators often belittle coaches, many lessons can be learned from sports coaches. This idea of mixed practice is common in professional training—including for teachers, novelists, police officers, and doctors. Their most profound learning experiences are embedded in mixed practice, sometimes in the form of apprenticeships, simulations, and clinical experiences. A novelist learns that good writing is more than a singular event of sitting down, gathering thoughts, researching, writing, and editing. Rather, a great essay or novel forms over time through mixed practice of researching, writing, and editing. For doctors, simulations provide an environment of mixed practice as they seek to diagnose a patient on the basis of various symptoms.

If you neglect the current readiness levels of your students, you may as well be teaching to wallpaper—teaching the same thing in the same way no matter who walks into your class. This is problematic on many levels. When your lessons provide shared experiences for students (e.g., inquiry-based learning, problem-based learning), it is much easier to differentiate your instruction based on the varied readiness of students. Varied practice and mixed practice allow you to adjust to students' differing needs. Students can select or be exposed to various approaches to studying problems, and the mixed practice allows greater or lesser emphasis to be placed on practicing the areas of greatest need. Mixed practice promotes durable learning because it requires time for rehearsal and processes that encourage consolidation of thoughts and ideas. Durable learning goes beyond mere factual knowledge (e.g., recall and recognition) and fosters deeper conceptual knowledge that requires an understanding of the interrelationships of concepts and ideas.

? *How can you begin to transition from more frequent mass/block practice with students to mixed practice? How will you communicate this change to your students? How will this begin to change homework and in-class assignments?*

TIP 5

Interactive, Thoughtful Learning

As an educator, it is highly likely that you have taken the Myers-Briggs Type Indicator (Myers, McCaulley, Quenk, & Hammer, 1998) or something similar. So, are you an extrovert or an introvert? Despite at least one-third of the population or more identifying with being an introvert, researchers continually show that public perception casts introversion as less desirable than extroversion, which frequently is described as being smarter, better looking, and more likeable (Cain, 2013). It is vital that we identify and address any bias that we may hold about our students (even subconsciously) because it may drastically limit our success as teachers. Regardless of public perception, many extraordinary individuals have identified with being an introvert—Isaac Newton, Albert Einstein, Steven Spielberg, J. K. Rowling, and Fredric Chopin (Cain, 2013). Realize that pure extroversion or introversion is extremely rare; instead, our personalities tend to reside along a continuum that leans in one direction more than the other. Although teachers and students exhibit varying levels of one or the other, teachers need to be adept at acknowledging and celebrating the personality types of all students in the classroom. Remember that introversion or extroversion tendencies can both be great. Just make sure that your instructional approaches celebrate both and not one at the expense of the other.

Extroverts gain emotional energy from other people and thus often seek larger social settings. These individuals frequently initiate conversations and easily engage others. In your classroom, the quintessential extroverts will raise their hands—sometimes even though they don't know the answer—just because they want to interact. Extroverts are often reprimanded for talking at inappropriate times. These students excel when brainstorming new ideas.

Introverts, on the other hand, would rather interact with one or two close friends than with a large group. In the classroom, they will prefer smaller group interactions rather than full-class activities; they see quiet time as an opportunity to think and reflect; they often listen and encourage others in groups; they tend not to like sudden change. Introverts can be very creative if given sufficient time, and they tend to think through the details.

Jung and others have said that there is no such thing as a pure introvert or a pure extrovert (Jung, 1971). However, it is important to realize that you and your students tend to be more comfortable with either the interpersonal (external social realm) or the intrapersonal (the world within). Additionally, a small percentage of individuals are ambiverts, falling in the middle of the introvert-extrovert personality continuum.

Taking a personality inventory to categorize a general tendency is easy, but the important thing is what we do with the label. For teaching professionals, that means learning when and where to be more extroverted and when and where to be more introverted. As we seek to engage and motivate students, it is important to seek a balance of introverted and extroverted tendencies. Some students will thrive in quieter one-on-one conversations while others prefer larger group interactions. Further, you have likely noticed that classrooms take on personalities as well. Some classes tend to be more reserved and quiet, and others tend to be more social and interactive.

A common notion is that we need to always try to cater to the natural tendencies and preferred learning modalities of our students. I suggest this is not always true. All students need to be confident communicators and thoughtful writers, so we need to help them learn to grow their strengths and improve their weaknesses. We can achieve this using a variety of strategies, but the goal is always to ensure that students are active participants in the learning, not passive recipients.

TIP 5 focuses on two questions: (1) How can you promote a culture of rich interactivity (*Culture of Interactivity*), and (2) Where does your lesson facilitate thoughtful, purposeful engagement (*Depth of Engagement*)?

TIP 5
Interactive, Thoughtful Learning

Score	1 (Needs Improvement)	3 (Proficient)	5 (Exemplary)
Culture of Interactivity (5a)	**Promotes culture of rich interactivity.**		
	Teacher does not actively involve students in the lesson; student participation is missing or rare.	Questioning stimulates participation and involvement of all students at various points in the lesson.	Questioning stimulates participation and involvement of all students consistently throughout lesson.
	No explicit interactions are facilitated between teacher and students or among peers; instruction discourages conversation, questions, or engagement.	Interactions facilitated are at times conversational, engaging, and/or motivating.	Interactions facilitated are consistently conversational, engaging, and motivating throughout entire lesson.
	All learning is either intrapersonal (individual) or interpersonal (collaborative); no balance seen.	Learning experiences provide balance of interpersonal (collaborative) and intrapersonal (individual) learning.	Additionally, interpersonal and intrapersonal learning is effectively timed and linked to the lesson.
Depth of Engagement (5b)	**Facilitates thoughtful, purposeful student engagement.**		
	Interactions and assignments lack explicit purpose and personal connection to students.	Interactions and assignments are purposeful (linked to key skills and/or knowledge) and personal (relevant, motivating, engaging to learner).	Additionally, students provide evidence of connections to personal applications through discussion, reflections, or other observable data.
	Interactions focus on one correct answer; typically short-answer responses are expected.	Interactions frequently challenge students to explain, reason, and/or justify thinking and solutions.	Additionally, students frequently critique the responses of other students and the teacher.

Culture of Interactivity

Classroom strategies and curriculum help to frame how lessons progress, but the questions we ask students and the ways we engage them are critical for motivating them. I commonly see students who are distant and disengaged in one classroom become engaged and lively in another. Why the difference? It could partially be that they prefer one discipline over another, but the culture created is also paramount to engaging and motivating learners.

One way to maximize engagement is to lower stress. Our society values high achievers, and although the effort to push students in that direction is well intended, it often results in students feeling enormous pressure to succeed at all costs. In reality, performance in and out of the classroom is best when the challenge is high but the pressure is low. When students feel safe taking risks and making mistakes, then they will, with proper guidance, challenge themselves in amazing ways. If, however, students fear failing, they will often avoid even trying so that they don't look dumb in front of their peers. After all, many students feel that they didn't really fail if they didn't try in the first place. This is an understandable defense mechanism. If participation from all students is the goal, then the culture needs to provide a safe and challenging yet low-stress environment.

? *How do you encourage participation from all students?*

Creating a culture of high participation may involve learning from others. Have you noticed that some individuals easily engage people, whereas others seem less able to do so? Those who succeed have an ability to demonstrate that they genuinely care about the person they are talking to, and they frequently ask engaging questions.

Think carefully about how you demonstrate that you care for all students. Or perhaps you have a tendency to show favoritism to some. Your self-perception in this area is not nearly as important as your students' perceptions. It is easy to find out what they think by administering a brief anonymous survey that will tell you whether their perceptions align with yours. You can include a simple multiple-choice question such as this: "Ms. X shows that she cares deeply about the success of each student (a) always and for all students, (b) for some students but not others, (c) rarely for any students."

Asking questions that generate interest and intrigue is a second aspect of engaging others. Closed-ended questions at the lower end of Bloom's taxonomy rarely generate conversations, nor do they provide motivation for students to explore further. Here are some examples: Who was the author of the story? What years did the Vietnam War occur? What are the parts of a flower? Instead we can begin with richer, more dynamic questions, such as these: What mood was the author trying to convey? What's the evidence for your answer? Sometimes an open-ended statement can help to begin conversations. Consider these examples: I am most curious to learn about ____; My greatest hope is ____; If I were in charge, I would change ____. Another option is to ask students what questions they have on topics to be studied. The overall goal is to create a climate of questioning, curiosity, and intrigue. Sharing things that students are curious about helps promote a conversational, interactive learning environment, which is far more productive than a didactic environment. Once students are engaged, we undoubtedly need to ask them some more mundane, factual questions, but if we start with those, then we risk never engaging students in the first place.

? *How can you facilitate purposeful conversations while motivating and engaging your students?*

At the start of this chapter I discussed the importance of becoming adept at working in both the interpersonal, collaborative world and the intrapersonal, reflective world—and this applies to teachers *and* students. Teachers must engage in the interpersonal world when interacting with parents, serving on committees, working with students, or being part of a department or grade level. They must navigate the intrapersonal realm when planning, reflecting, creating, and analyzing. Both are essential elements that collectively lead to success as a teacher. Likewise, students need to collaborate on projects as they develop their interpersonal skills, but they also need to reflect on their progress or demonstrate individual achievement during the intrapersonal aspects of learning.

It is important to help students who struggle with interpersonal interactions to develop this skill instead of enabling them to avoid it. After all, individuals are often fired from their jobs because of their inability to work well with others. Allow opportunities for shy or introverted students to share thoughts and ideas in smaller groups instead of in front of the entire class. As students become more comfortable interacting with others, provide opportunities for them to share in front of the entire class, but with the support of other group members.

The intrapersonal aspects of learning are equally critical for success. As students learn to become more self-reflective or metacognitive, they begin to model an important aspect of lifelong learning. Further, by understanding what their strengths and weaknesses are, they can begin to frame questions to help them resolve difficulties they are having in writing, problem-solving, or study habits. Think-pair-share is a great strategy to promote students' development of both the interpersonal and the intrapersonal aspects of learning, because it involves the intrapersonal (think) and the interpersonal (share), linked by a combination of both (pair). Using guided questions to help students reflect on their learning at the end of the share component deepens their learning and makes it more personal—think-pair-share becomes think-pair-share-think. For instance, after students have shared information or ideas as a class, they could be asked to reflect in their journals or notebooks by responding to questions such as these: What do you still find confusing? What step is most difficult?

? *Where in your lessons do you provide opportunities for students to engage in both interpersonal (collaborative) interactions and intrapersonal (individual, reflective) learning experiences?*

Depth of Engagement

The famous struggle between Apollo and Dionysus, cited in Dante's *Inferno*, is the age-old battle between mind and heart—each seemingly wants something different. Likewise, what is purposeful and personal differs from student to student. As with most everything in life, balance and variety are key. Using Dante's example, learning becomes more personal for all when it involves both the mind and the heart, not just one or the other.

To make learning personal, you can link it to hobbies, sports, art, or music. And you can motivate and engage students through problems, questions, and challenges that have significance for them. For example, in high school, topics related to driving a car could be incorporated into essay writing, or math or physics problems. For elementary students, things that are tangible and part of everyday life can be the personal hook that engages them. Reading a story about a dog or a cousin, for example, may lead students to announce that they have a dog or a cousin and make them eager to share. In middle schools, relationships make for interesting topics, as long as discussions do not get too personal, cross the line of appropriateness, or cause embarrassment.

When direct connections to students' lives are not possible, make sure that the learning is nevertheless purposeful. Consider, for example, how you might reference a significant global issue, such as high unemployment, insufficient clean water, political and social instability, or severe income disparities. Even if you find it challenging to relate such issues to a specific standard, your goal should be to find a way to bring the topic closer to home for students. For instance, I was recently in a social studies class where the majority of students indicated that they would be perfectly fine with government limits on their First Amendment right to freedom of speech. Based on how the issue was presented, I was not surprised by the outcome of the student vote. If the question had been related to something they valued, the vote likely would have been different. Specifically, if the government limited the type of music students could listen to or prevented students from speaking in public until they were 16, then perhaps they would see freedom of speech very differently.

? *How do you ensure that your lessons are purposeful and personal for students?*

Before students can explain, reason, model, or justify their reasoning or thinking, they need an appropriate prompt. In math, for example, asking students to read aloud short-answer responses from a worksheet or share their solutions to last night's math problems limits their thinking, engagement, and ability to be more analytical about their work. Far more effective are probing questions from the teacher, such as "Are there other ways it could be solved or written? Did anyone solve it differently?"

The selection of problems and how they are addressed are also important. If the homework assignment was to work 20 similar problems, then the goal was likely to practice computational fluency on a certain topic. You may need to model—or, better yet, have the students model—the solution for only 5 of the 20 problems. You can simply post the answers to the others. When students work problems on the board, be efficient with time. Have some students work at the board while others check their answers to the other problems, or have a student place his paper under the document camera for others to see and discuss. In most classrooms a lot of time is wasted when students work at the board as the others watch. You can also have students use small erasable marker boards on which they write solutions on the left side and a verbal explanation on the right side. This approach encourages communication of thought processes and provides a way to practice written expression. In language arts classes, students can share thesis statements or best examples, and then others can critique the work to make it stronger, clearer, or more concise.

? *Under what conditions will your students be challenged to explain, reason, or justify their thinking during the next lesson or two?*

Actions for TIP 5

To guide your discussions, self-reflection, and next steps, consider the following actions that address the central concepts for TIP 5: *Culture of Interactivity* and *Depth of Engagement.*

Action: Construct Engaging Questions

How did your questioning engage your students over the past few days? Did you provide a scenario, share something from current events, propose a dilemma, or focus on something students have been asking? Consider the questions shown in the table on page 76. Some seek to engage students in participating, and others are designed to just teach content. As I plan a new lesson, my default approach starts with mundane, less engaging questions (like those in the right column); but then I rework them until I have found the hook or means to engage the learner. Caution: Don't go into class tomorrow and just start asking participatory questions if you've only used content-focused questions up to now. Scaffolding is needed to help students learn to tackle challenging, engaging questions. The questions that we ask guide the level of rigor students undertake, and they may need support to shift to new, higher levels.

? *What are three questions that you asked during the past two days that stimulated participation and that also addressed key content or process? How can you improve these questions? What are several questions that you will ask students in the days ahead to deeply engage them in participation? How will you help to scaffold this change in your class?*

Participatory Versus Content-Focused Questions

Discipline (topic)	Questions Designed to Increase Participation	Questions to Elicit Content
Social Studies (Causes of war)	• Have you ever had a major disagreement with a sibling or a friend? What happened and how was the situation resolved? • Is war ever justified? Explain.	What were the causes of the Civil War? The Vietnam War? The American Revolutionary War?
Math (Area)	• The local pizza place is offering two medium (12-inch) pizzas for $12 or one large (16-inch) pizza for $12. Which is the better deal and why? If you don't eat the outer 1½ inches (crust) of either pizza, is the answer still the same?	Given the formula, what is the area of a circle with a radius of 7?
English/Language Arts (Elements of effective writing)	• Identify a well-written sentence (choosing an example from books, articles, websites, music lyrics) and justify your opinion as to why it is so well written. Write the best sentence you can for at least two of the following: marketing your favorite product, making a convincing claim, offering an apology.	Write a paragraph on the following topic: _____.
Science (Newton's Laws of Motion)	• Model/draw all the pushes and pulls exerted on you at various times when you ride a roller coaster, when you are in a car accident, or when you ride on a spaceship (pick one).	What are Newton's Three Laws of Motion? Give an example of each.

Action: Frame Conversations Around *How* and *Why*

Many classes are mired in *what* questions that typically elicit a one-word response. When the answer is correct, we acknowledge and move on; when it's incorrect, we provide a correct response or seek the correct answer from another student, acknowledge, and move on. Then we appear dumbfounded when students show little interest, are apathetic, sleep in class, are disruptive, or stare at us blankly.

To have classrooms that are conversational, motivating, and engaging, we have to construct the stage where this can occur. One way to do this is by asking more *how* and *why* questions to get students talking. This means going beyond a focus on single facts, isolated concepts, or solitary skills to be memorized; it does not mean that *what* questions are not valuable. For instance, *what* questions that require students to explain, elaborate, or justify their answer can be very powerful. The goal is to avoid a didactic, two-person game that excludes the other 20 or 30 students in the room. Opt for questions that cause students to react, think, explore, and share their ideas.

Instead of asking students to read a sentence and choose the correct singular or plural verb form, provide several sentences and have students find where errors occurred, justifying any edits. This example highlights subject-verb agreement, but the assignment could include other errors that are common in writing. Remember the discussion of TIP 4 about how mixed or interleaved practice is more valuable and more engaging than single-focus repetition? Think about it—an editor does not go through a manuscript looking only for subject-verb agreement and then reread looking only for passive voice or coherence. As discussed earlier, the interleaved-practice approach also provides opportunities for differentiation in classrooms.

In science, *how* and *why* questions can help students to better understand and explain the natural world around them. In mathematics, you could ask a more routine problem (solve for x: $3x - y = 7$ and then graph the line), or you could put students in groups, provide them with meter sticks, stopwatches, and graph paper, and ask them to graph a specific motion shown by the teacher or another student (e.g., walk at a constant rate or walk at a uniformly increasing speed). Both problems address equations of lines, graphing, and slope, but only the second problem challenges students to engage in observing, measuring, and analyzing, not just calculating. Yes, practice problems will be necessary to develop computational fluency, but these should be worked after students are engaged.

? *How do you currently engage your students in conversations? How can you improve these discussions? How and where in the lesson do you locate the more mundane practice of skills and content?*

Action: Move from Self-Centered to Idea-Centered Learning

It is normal for children up to age 6 to be self-centered in their thinking and learning. Piaget would call this egocentrism. However, in grades 2 and beyond, students have the ability to appreciate the viewpoint of others. Yet our education processes generally fail to develop this skill. I base this statement on my regular visits to classrooms around the country, and, specifically, on a recent sampling of 40 classroom observations in various K–12 school settings. In those observations, only 4 teachers (10 percent) had students interacting and building on the ideas of others. In the other 36 classrooms, students either worked only with their own thoughts and ideas or responded in a didactic exchange with only the teacher. With slight changes, these egocentric classrooms could evolve into idea-centric classrooms where students discuss ideas and thoughts regardless of whether the initial questions are their own or someone else's.

A quick way to check to see if your classroom is egocentric is to observe how frequently students state the same thought as another student without even realizing it; or you can listen to determine how often they ask the same or similar questions. When classrooms become more idea-centric, students begin expanding their knowledge—building on ideas, thoughts, and questions from their peers.

An English language arts class might begin with dissecting an author's sentence. Groups of students can work to improve the sentence, and then the class can come together to generate a series of sentences that are better written. In math, if students do not agree on an answer, they can try to figure out how each of the different solutions was determined. This activity requires students to look at all the possibilities and try to figure out where errors may have occurred. Once they do this, they will be more likely to provide a correct solution with confidence. In this example, the teacher does not indicate which solution is correct until students consider the various possibilities. When they begin to take more ownership of their solutions, they become less dependent on the teacher and more reliant on themselves and their peers. This characteristic illustrates a lifelong learner—not someone playing the game of school.

? *What changes can you begin to make to create more idea-centric classes? How can you gradually make this part of normal learning?*

Action: Increase Purpose and Relevance

During my first year of teaching physics, I took great pride in seamlessly deriving the needed equations while I solved and modeled solutions to problems for my students. However, my pride was quickly stifled when a few weeks into the course a very bright student came into class and asked, "Are you going to throw spaghetti on the board again today?" A little perplexed by his statement, I asked him to elaborate. He explained that when I worked physics problems, the outcome often looked like a big bowl of spaghetti had been randomly thrown on the board. Humbled, I began to rethink my teaching and realized that effective teaching wasn't about me displaying my knowledge so much as it was about engaging students in learning experiences that are personal and purposeful.

I've made the point previously that any time that we can tie a lesson, a problem, or a topic to the music, sports, or other interests of our students, the learning becomes more personal. This is not about trying to become "cooler" by inserting teen slang into our speaking, as though we were one of them. Students need role models more than they need another peer. However, when we show an interest in their world, they quickly become more attuned to our class and our goals. Sometimes this can be as easy as adding students' names to math problems, or adding mention of a popular music group or song into a discussion in a literacy circle.

Engaging the emotions is another means to grab student attention. Think about some of the classes or experiences that stand out most vividly from your past experience. There was likely a significant emotional aspect to these events. Further, think about the last time you purchased something major—emotions probably played a role. Marketing companies spend millions to get us to associate a positive emotion with their company or product. Robert Plutchik (2001) developed an emotion wheel that identifies and categorizes 24 emotions, ranging from joy and trust to anger and boredom. Remember, of course, that even though emotions such as fear can help to make things memorable, the goal is to build *positive* emotional connections for students. (When I was a student, my 9th grade geometry class was built around fear; the teacher would ask us to stand and recite the theorem or postulate, and embarrassment would follow for those who did not remember.) We want to challenge and engage learners by developing a positive culture around feelings such as trust, interest, and intrigue.

TIP 6 will focus more heavily on curiosity, creativity, and intrigue, but it suffices to say that bringing the outside world of music to an English class, global challenges to an economics lesson, or real data sets to a math or science class gives learning purpose and relevance. Wouldn't you be more engaged in a class that begins with a question like "Can you predict tomorrow's weather" instead of a stated objective like "You will be able to interpret the symbols found on a weather map"? Wouldn't you rather write a personal letter to a favorite author, musician, or other personality than learn by rote the steps for how to write a personal letter? In each case, the goals are the same, but the engagement factor is totally different. Students can propose how they might predict the weather or draft a letter without knowing all the content or having all the necessary skills. In fact, they will quickly discover and frequently begin to ask for more details, information, or resources to help achieve their goal. Imagine that—a class where students are asking you for information and details regarding things that they *want* to know.

? *How can you better appeal to the emotional side of your students? Generate a list of various ways that you can connect your curriculum to your students' lives over the next few weeks. How are you attempting to connect to your most challenging and disengaged students?*

Action: Increase Expectations by Asking Students to Explain, Reason, and Justify

How questions are framed determines whether the response will be of a lower or higher order, superficial or deep, factual or nuanced. Questions like "Why do you think that?" "How do you know this?" and "How could we figure this out?" exemplify how to encourage deeper thinking and challenge students. In contrast, common questions like "Does everyone understand?" and "What questions do you still have?" do not elicit the outcome that we hope for. These latter examples tend to be transitional questions rather than questions that promote rich, thoughtful learning. Asking "What questions do you still have?" usually draws responses only from students who were going to ask a question anyway.

Think about modifying vague or transitional questions to generate responses that are more metacognitive—requiring students to think about their thinking. For instance, change "Does everyone understand?" to "Tell your neighbor or write in your journal where you are most confused or which step is most confusing." In addition to promoting metacognition, this change can also help to narrow the achievement gap. Vague or generic questions such as "Does everyone understand?" typically generate responses from the more academically successful kids. Kids who are lost do not know where to begin asking questions, nor do they feel comfortable doing so. Getting all students to focus on areas of challenge helps develop a study skill that many low-achieving students lack.

? *When did you recently challenge students to think more deeply about their work by having them explain or justify? How can you make this a more consistent part of practice? How can you make it more of an expectation for your students?*

TIP 6

Creative, Problem-Solving Culture

Curiosity is the insatiable desire to explore, and it begins at a very early age. Unfortunately, for many students, something tends to quell that desire as they progress through school. Perhaps it's because our schools often reward students for knowing facts instead of applauding them for posing questions and seeking solutions. With the assistance of high-stakes tests, schools have moved from being places of challenge and curiosity to places that promote simplistic thinking and recall of unconnected facts. Leonardo da Vinci, Thomas Edison, Albert Einstein, and Philo Farnsworth all provide extraordinary representations of extremely curious thinkers. Their thinking and questioning occurred by integrating science, engineering, and, in some cases, art. (By the way, aren't you at least a little curious to know who Philo Farnsworth was?)

Creative thinking spans every domain of learning and every career path from architecture and fine arts to economics and entrepreneurialism. So what is our role as teacher or mentor in guiding and encouraging curiosity and creativity among all our students? We can do many things, but a critical starting point is to approach teaching and learning like a puzzle or a mystery to be solved rather than facts to be memorized and restated on a quiz or a test. Beyond the TIP 4 discussion about challenge and high expectations is the need to seek a balance in creating an environment that encourages curiosity and creativity while also ensuring that students learn essential facts, core content, and key ideas.

Generally speaking, curiosity is a response to an information gap. Curiosity increases when there's a gap between what we know and what we would like to know. When the gap is too small, curiosity languishes because the solution appears trivial; when it is too large, curiosity dissipates because the solution seems beyond our current ability. In this sense, curiosity aligns with Vygotsky's zone of proximal development (1978), where maximal creativity occurs because the information gap and our confidence are at a moderate, not an extreme, level—a "just right" zone. The teacher's goal thus becomes finding the appropriate zone for each student.

We know that schools primarily test cognitive or intellectual abilities, but these abilities only partially account for future success. For instance, the personality traits of conscientiousness and curiosity account for just as much as intelligence or general cognitive abilities when it comes to future success (Leslie, 2014). Ultimately, it seems that one of a teacher's greatest roles is to model and guide students' curiosity in ways that increase motivation as they explore what-ifs. Of course, factual knowledge remains important, but classroom environments that promote curiosity and creativity make factual knowledge a means to an end and not an end in itself.

TIP 6 focuses primarily on two questions: (1) How do you foster and encourage a creative and inquisitive learning environment (*Creative Culture*), and (2) How do you provide learning experiences that encourage creativity and problem solving (*Problem-Solving Environment*)?

Creative Culture

To be creative, imaginative, and innovative, we have to be willing to take risks. However, taking risks often requires that we confront fears—fears of failure and anxiety about the unknown.

I have always been struck by how each class takes on a different personality. For example, a high school chemistry class I taught in 1990 was a unique class that frustrated me greatly, but it was not until many years later that I realized the cause of my frustration—which was not what you might expect. The students were well behaved, were not mean or cruel, and did their work when asked. But none of them were willing to take risks—at all. As a result, the class flowed without incident, but also without a pulse. These students played everything safe, generating no energy or curiosity whatsoever. They came to class, did their assignments, but creativity, questioning, or innovation were completely absent. They demonstrated no desire to know anything about the world around them. For them, education seemed to boil down to nothing more than completing assignments, getting a good grade, and going to a good college.

TIP 6
Creative, Problem-Solving Culture

Score	1 (Needs Improvement)	3 (Proficient)	5 (Exemplary)
Creative Culture (6a)	**Fosters creative, inquisitive learning environment.**		
	Students are expected to give knowledge back in same form it was presented.	Creativity in expressing thoughts and ideas is encouraged. Teacher models creative approaches.	Students are expected to find novel ways to communicate, share, present, and/or discuss ideas and are praised for doing so.
	Student curiosity and questioning are stifled by teacher actions.	Culture perpetuates and encourages student curiosity and questioning.	Curiosity and questioning are prevalent during multiple aspects of the lesson.
Problem-Solving Environment (6b)	**Provides learning experiences that encourage creativity and problem solving.**		
	No open-ended problems are studied. Students only learn to mimic teacher.	Teacher creates environment where students seek solutions to open-ended problems.	Additionally, students are fairly self-directed in their quest for solutions, and open-ended problems are complex and/or multi-stepped.
	Lesson focuses on single perspective/solution with no student creativity allowed or encouraged.	Teacher presents lessons that provide opportunities for considering multiple perspectives and alternate solutions/explanations.	Students actively consider multiple perspectives and offer alternative solutions/explanations without teacher prompting.
	Everything is defined/told before students explore/question/observe (algorithm, definitions, or explanation all precede experience); or there is no exploration at all.	Teacher facilitates student exploration of major concepts/ideas before formal explanation occurs.	Additionally, students take active role in designing how the exploration will occur.

As I reflect on this group, I wonder what most of them are doing in life and whether they're still playing it safe. To me, life becomes exciting when we venture into the unknown and the unexpected and try things that we have never done before. Whether people choose to become a choreographer, a venture capitalist, a stay-at-home dad, a lawyer, or a research scientist, those who excel will be those who are willing to question, to ask "what if," or to think about how things can be different or better—all of which demand creativity, persistence, and willingness to confront fears and anxieties.

I always tell my students that the classroom is a safe place to fail. Further, I tell them that as they learn and grow, I want them to try things that they have not tried before. When the test rolls around, I want them to succeed, not fail; but sometimes they will stumble early on in their effort to grow. If every day is potentially punitive, with everything graded either correct or incorrect, then students will never want to take risks— unless they don't care about grades in the first place. Perhaps we have been doing things backward for a long time. Instead of seeking ways to avoid errors during the process of learning, maybe we should be celebrating them, because sometimes learning involves growing from our errors, provided we are willing to recognize them and work to improve. What is the best error that you have recently made?

? *How do you encourage creative thinking in your students?*

Promoting curiosity and encouraging questioning are among the expectations related to the newer standards. For instance, the Common Core State Standards for English language arts require students to integrate, infer, and make connections. In mathematics, students are required to interpret, extend, and compare. In science, students must be able to model, create, and design. If these standards are to be achieved, then students must become creative and curious. In the process, creative thinking skills can enhance student content mastery (Beghetto & Kaufman, 2010).

Likewise, the College Board, which develops advanced placement courses and exams, has begun to revise all 36 courses. Key changes focus on covering fewer topics and emphasizing creative, deeper thinking over rote memorization.

None of these changes in standards or expectations is about getting rid of content knowledge. Instead, they represent a shift from focusing primarily or solely on the *what*. Now, the *what* needs to be integrated into the *how* and the *why*.

? *What does a culture of curiosity and questioning look like in your classroom? What steps need to be taken to improve it?*

Problem-Solving Environment

How do the questions and problems provided in a typical math class differ from those in a TIP-proficient math class? In the typical class, the teacher provides students with the algorithm, models several similar problems, and then gives students time to practice what they have been told and shown. In a TIP-proficient classroom, students are provided problems such as the following, which deals with the concept of area:

> Which is the better deal—1 large 14-inch pizza for $10 or 2 medium 10-inch pizzas for $10? Extend: If you never eat your crust (the outer 1 inch of a pizza), would your answer remain the same? Explain.

After reaching the solution, students would still need practice in solving additional problems involving area, but the point is that the problem shown here requires students to go beyond just calculating area; they must interpret solutions and compare which option is a better value. In another example, a TIP-proficient teacher might provide students with a floor plan of different-sized rooms and ask them to figure out not only how much carpet would be needed if it comes in rolls that are 8 feet wide, but also how carpet seams and the overall cost to minimize.

We often think of problem solving as relegated only to mathematics, but all fields involve problem solving. Think of writers, historians, and scientists, among others. The writer might have to determine how to present a convincing argument within a 250-word limit. The historian might analyze how great figures in history achieved their power and gained a following. The scientist, knowing that the EPA has determined that a hazardous chemical is safe to drink if it is diluted to 1 part per million, might need to calculate how many gallons of water are necessary to render the chemical relatively harmless if 55 gallons of it were spilled into a lake.

? *How do your upcoming lessons provide opportunities for students to tackle complex, open-ended problems?*

Real-world problems usually involve numerous perspectives and have various possible solutions. When a student or parent tells me about a certain situation, I have learned to gather as much information as possible from everyone involved. What inevitably happens is that all the accounts contain some truth, but each individual's perspective has a certain amount of subjectivity. For instance, if a student turns and walks away from someone, many inferences can be made: (1) the student was upset and wanted to snub the other person, so she turned and left; (2) the student heard her name, so she turned to see who was calling her; or (3) the student just remembered that she left her homework assignment in her last class, so she went to get it. Although better communication from the student would have been preferred, many reactions or perceptions may be warranted from the same observation. The other person could (1) be offended, (2) see that the student was distracted by someone else, or (3) understand the situation after realizing that the student needed to get something quickly. Often we don't get all the information, which makes it difficult to accurately assess the situation.

Learning is similar. History, for example, often presents things from a male perspective, an immigant's perspective, a leader's perspective, or the teacher's perspective instead of considering multiple perspectives—those of a business person, a local citizen, a slave, a woman—and loses the power of multiple perspectives. Studying a historic event from a single perspective can diminish the richness of the event and make it more likely that the information is inaccurate or potentially misleading. Therefore it is important for students to learn from multiple perspectives. In science, they can test hypotheses multiple times to ensure that the results are reliable and accurate, and then expand the conditions to see if the results are generalizable to other situations. In literature, they can explore various interpretations of a literary work. In expository writing, students can write a paragraph from various points of view. In each case, learning becomes a puzzle with many pieces, each contributing to the larger whole.

? *When will your students have opportunities during this week to consider multiple perspectives or alternate solutions?*

Teachers have many available tools and strategies, ranging from those that are very teacher centered to those that are very student centered. If the desire is to improve students' motivation and engagement, then student-centered learning approaches should be the preferred option. At the crux of most student-centered learning is the idea that students need to be able to explore and engage with the material before the teacher provides formal explanations or algorithms. This is true whether the instructional focus is inquiry based, project based, or problem based.

Be forewarned that switching from teacher as teller to teacher as facilitator requires a shift of culture in the classroom—not just a change in instructional approach. Instantly moving from telling students everything to asking them what *they* think will be met with frustration, resistance, and perhaps even anger. And why not? You have changed the rules without sharing the new rulebook with your students. Numerous resources are available to help teachers (and students) transition toward a more engaging, inquiry-based classroom (e.g., Marshall, 2013).

Successful guided inquiry-based instruction has two critical components. The first consists of changing the paradigm for how most lessons and activities are presented: instead of the teacher telling and then confirming, the students engage in doing and exploring before the summary, meaning making, or formal explanation of concepts. The second major component involves rethinking classroom management so that student talking, questioning, and exploring are encouraged, not subdued. Although inquiry-based instruction and other student-centered approaches are not the easiest option, their value, when done proficiently, can be substantial. To support this claim, Paulo Blikstein from Stanford University reports a controlled study that found a 25 percent increase in performance when exploration came before the text or video rather than after it (Dreifus, 2013). Further, effective inquiry-based instruction has been shown to promote higher proficiency among all groups tested (based on gender, race, ability level) when compared to typical instructional practice (Marshall & Alston, 2014).

? *How do you reverse the typical instructional sequence so that students explore concepts before you provide a formal explanation?*

Actions for TIP 6

To guide your discussions, self-reflection, and next steps, consider the following actions that address the central chapter foci for TIP 6: *Creative Culture* and *Problem-Solving Environment*.

Action: Promote Creative Thought with an "Hourglass" Approach to Learning

Whether the subject is Newton's Laws of Motion, World War II, expository writing, or the Pythagorean Theorem, teachers typically deliver the information and then allow students time to practice with the already known idea. What child—or adult, for that matter—is curious and excited about coming into class knowing that today she will be learning about mitosis (cell division), memorizing the stages of mitosis, and then looking at a few slides that show cells in various stages of mitosis? The likelihood of that happening is slim. Instead, most of us are curious, in school and in life, when there is information, a story, a contradiction, or other element that makes us want to know more. Learning about how a single zygote (sperm and egg) becomes a complex human being should be extremely fascinating and generate all sorts of questions; it should not be a series of terms to learn and memorize in a vacuum, with no context to engage the learner.

Before radio broadcaster Paul Harvey's death in 2009, I recall being captivated by his program *The Rest of the Story*. He would begin by telling the background story of a famous person, event, or thing, and although it was often possible to figure out the "mystery" along the way, Harvey never shared the actual or recognized name of the person, event, or thing until the very end. His storytelling manner acted much like a funnel, starting broadly with many details and bits of background information, and then working its way down the channeled sides until reaching the final narrow opening.

This is how a good mystery works; this is how science works; this is how effective and highly engaging learning works. However, if creativity and innovation are your goals, don't stop with the discovery of the law, the full understanding of the plot, or the understanding of the historical event. Rather, continue to go further, asking the "so what," the "now what," or the "what can we do now" questions. Learning then becomes like an hourglass, as you focus and channel students' thinking to a clear conclusion, a focused idea, or a realization, but then extend their understanding by asking them to apply it, generalize it, or improve it in some way.

? *What story can you tell that will engage students in questioning events or the world around them? How can you begin to flip the way the content is studied so that its real purpose and value are clear from the beginning, not presented as an afterthought or as time allows?*

Action: Plan "FedEx Days" to Encourage Curiosity and Creativity

One way to encourage students to think and behave in creative ways is to plan a "FedEx Day," when you give them time to think about, read about, or experiment with something that they are curious about and then share what they discovered over the course of their investigation. This idea comes from Mike Cannon-Brookes, cofounder of an Australian software company, and is featured in Daniel Pink's *Drive* (2009). Employees at Cannon-Brookes' firm are periodically given 24 hours to work on any project that they desire, and the results are "delivered" the next day. In a classroom context, students may initially struggle with the freedom to openly explore their ideas, but it is an opportunity to motivate and engage students through the pursuit of creative endeavors. You can begin by helping students brainstorm possible questions to explore during the first five minutes of class, and then turn them loose. The goal is to create opportunities for students to pursue, test, explore, and discover in nonprescriptive ways. You might begin by scheduling a FedEx Day once a quarter and then increase frequency as the year progresses.

Psychologist Ellis Paul Torrance (1987) developed tests of creative thinking that scored creativity in five domains, including originality and elaboration (the others are fluency, abstractness of titles, and resistance to premature closure). As you attempt to help students become nimble, flexible thinkers, it is likely that originality will be a particular challenge until they begin to develop a larger vocabulary, more content knowledge, and expanded skill sets. Peter Thiel, cofounder of PayPal, would agree that true originality is challenging to achieve. In his book *From Zero to One* (2014), he contends that true innovation is about creating a new singular event, "0 to 1." However, much of what is considered innovative today is simply a modification or scaling up of a previously existing idea, "1 to n." Getting students to increase their competence relative to the domain of elaboration is helpful in improving writing skills, making conclusions, working with data, or sorting through historical facts. Which domain of creativity you focus upon is not nearly as important as simply encouraging students to think outside the realm of expected responses—particularly when those responses are usually in the form of a single word or a single correct solution.

? *When and where do students have the opportunity to be creative in your class? If you had a FedEx Day, what would you model for students as* *your attempt at creativity? Remember that if you ask students to take risks, their trust will be much greater if they see you taking a risk as well.*

Action: Recognize and Reward Risk by Encouraging Open-Ended Learning

What? Recognizing and rewarding *risk*? We don't want our students indiscriminately engaging in taking risks. However, the point is to encourage students to transition from simply mimicking the teacher to instead thinking, acting, and responding to challenging questions, complex scenarios, or general curiosities.

Earlier I discussed bringing real-world issues into the classroom, and the point is relevant here. To engage students in seeking solutions to open-ended problems, consider tackling a significant global or community issue that you can link to your discipline. Examples include access to clean water, sustainable development in the face of population increases, education for all, and the gap between rich and poor. The Millennium Project (http://www.millennium-project.org) provides many great scenarios that can be used to begin conversations with your students, and they are applicable in a variety of classes. In English language arts, students can develop persuasive essays supporting their research; in social studies, they can explore how past and present societies have addressed these issues—and how future societies might do so; and in math class, they can look at trends, exponential growth (or decline), and financial expenses associated with solving complex problems.

If tackling a global challenge seems like too much for starters, consider this possibility instead. Tell students: "Your assignment for tomorrow is to bring to class a question or curiosity that you have that is related to the unit we're studying." This approach ties learning to student interests and makes the experience more relevant. Although students may find the assignment challenging at first, it will get easier as they see examples from others.

? *How can you get students to bring real-world questions into your class that relate to your content? How can you better tie the real world to your students' experiences? What resources can you consult when you have difficulty relating your content to the real world?*

Action: Offer Multiple Perspectives

When we provide scenarios, case studies, and problem-based or project-based learning experiences, we provide opportunities for multiple perspectives or solutions. If learning is about stating facts (2 x 2 = 4; there are 50 states in the United States; *with* is a preposition), then multiple perspectives or solutions are either unnecessary or impossible. However, many of the meaningful questions or experiences in school and life are less absolute and cannot be addressed simply by conducting a Google search. A study in a forensics science class, for example, could lead to multiple solutions that need to be defended.

Good group projects that involve case studies or rich problems need balance—that is, they should be enough to require the efforts of many while not totally overwhelming any one student in the process. In good collaborative projects, students should realize that *our* ideas always exceed *my* ideas alone!

? *How can you reword today's lesson to include complex problems that have multiple solution paths? How do you ensure that the content learned is still rigorous when students engage in project-based, problem-based learning, or inquiry-based learning?*

Action: Promote Explore Before Explain— and Save the Punch Line for Last

If you are like most teachers, it is quite possible that your instructional approach—one that has been the norm for decades—has been backward. That is, you tell first and then you ask students to restate the new knowledge or practice using it. You tell students about photosynthesis, the Spanish-American War, prepositional phrases, or proportional reasoning, and then you ask them to use the knowledge in a sentence or in a set of problems.

Although this approach may have worked in the past and was appropriate for the goals at the time, it won't work in addressing the new demands for today's learners. (Further, it is just plain boring.) Now that standards require students to analyze ideas, model complex phenomena, and create evidence-based arguments, they need to explore ideas before you provide the formal explanation.

This shift requires a rethinking of how you teach and your purpose for teaching. Current instruction is predicated on telling the punch line before the joke. This doesn't work for standup comedy, and it doesn't work for solid instruction that requires deep thinking. Allowing students to wrestle with new problems before showing them a solution promotes greater learning. Specifically, asking students to explore before you explain creates a need for them to learn, to be creative, and to think deeply.

? *What were three recent opportunities that you provided for students to explore before you explained the major concept? How can you make this approach more the norm instead of the exception? If you do this regularly, how can you deepen students' explorations? How can the paradigm be flipped so that exploration precedes explanation?*

TIP 7

Monitoring, Assessment, and Feedback That Guide and Inform Instruction and Learning

Perhaps nowhere in education is the stress greater for teachers, leaders, and students than in the issues surrounding high-stakes assessments and teacher evaluation. An enormous amount of time is devoted to the preparation and administration of high-stakes tests. Teacher performance in many states is now largely determined by student success on key assessments. Schools and districts are identified as thriving or barely surviving based on these assessments. This book doesn't seek to advocate for or rail against any current state or federal mandates; instead, it seeks to help teachers and leaders improve what takes place in the classroom during all the other days of the year when high-stakes tests are not being given. To be clear, major summative assessments, which include state testing, do not significantly improve teaching or learning. Their point is to provide a static, point-in-time assessment of how well students and grade levels have mastered a set of measurable objectives—not to inform teaching and learning for today or tomorrow.

Much like a global-positioning phone app, assessments associated with learning essentially entail three major components: (1) starting point, (2) best route (sometimes with optional routes to choose from), and (3) final destination. Specifically, diagnostic assessments help identify the learner's starting point, which includes prior knowledge and misconceptions held. Formative assessments then help to inform and guide the learning during the "trip." Finally, summative assessments let us know the relative degree of success in making it to the final destination. Although summative assessments can be informative (in terms of informing instruction for the following year), their purpose is to confirm what has or has not happened. Once students have taken summative assessments, their learning is essentially finished, and the focus shifts to the score or grade rather than the learning.

To dramatically affect learning, focus needs to be aimed at the diagnostic and formative assessments that take place during daily instruction. If we ensure that solid teaching and learning occur throughout the year, supported with continual diagnostic and formative assessments, then the summative performances (and tests) will take care of themselves. Perhaps if we change our focus toward assessment *for* learning (formative) instead of assessment *of* learning (summative), we will feel less compelled to devote so much energy to reviewing and teaching to the final test and instead focus on actual learning.

I am always amazed at how frequently teachers are surprised by the performance—often poor—of their students on summative tests. A summative test should be confirmatory and not a lottery with unexpected results. Surprise usually indicates one of two things. Either the teacher did not provide enough formative checks along the way to know what her students know and are able to do, or the test did not represent what they learned. Sometimes students will experience the skills and content during learning in a very different form (e.g., using different vocabulary) than what appears on the actual test. This may occur if the teacher develops the lesson and then gives a publisher-generated test; or if students conduct a lab and then are given a traditional test without scaffolding their knowledge to a different format; or if the class is taught using primarily lower-order forms of thinking (recall, define, list) and then students are tested primarily on higher-order forms of thinking (compare/contrast, model, analyze). Each of these experiences is no different than a coach practicing (daily instruction) *basketball* skills all week with her athletes and then sending them out to compete in a *volleyball* match (summative test). They did not develop the competencies, nor show mastery of the essential skills, before they were tested.

In Hattie's review of more than 800 meta-analyses (2009), two instructional practices repeatedly show a strong effect on student achievement when effectively implemented: (1) providing specific and meaningful feedback to students, and (2) regularly embedding formative assessment into daily instructional practice. On the surface, these findings may suggest that we need more assessments, despite the signs of assessment fatigue related to all the standardized tests currently administered to students. However, when feedback is appropriately given and used to scaffold learning, and when formative assessments are used to guide teaching and learning, then we are able to modify instruction to maximize student success.

One practice that is not helpful is the increasingly common tendency to allow students to take tests again—an effort that can often take up considerable time before, during, or after school. Prolific or large-scale retesting seems to be missing the central problem—students were not ready to take the test/quiz/summative assessment in the first place, so retesting is little more than a bandage on a much larger problem.

Let's be honest. Even the best test is not perfect. Assessments are difficult to do well, so it is important to provide variety and continually reassess the quality of the assessments we use. During my first year of teaching, I was adamant that students earned what they earned. A student who earned 89.2 percent got a *B* (when 90.0 percent and above was considered an *A*). After all, students had extra-credit opportunities to earn more points. However, as I learned more about the relative accuracy or inaccuracy of my assessments—and assessments in general—in measuring the goals and objectives for my class, I realized that even the best assessments are not accurate down to plus or minus 1 percent (or even close). This humbling realization caused me to rethink how grades were earned and awarded in my class. Adding to my humility, I learned that item creation for any major standardized test (e.g., ACT, SAT, NAEP) takes about two years, including time for the item to be written, piloted, validated, and so forth. We might be tempted to say that we can't ever know with any certainty how well a student masters or understands anything, but the two-year time line goes too far to the other extreme.

TIP 7 focuses on two primary questions: (1) How well do your assessments measure and support student learning (*Feedback Guiding Learning*), and (2) What do formative assessments tell you about student progress relative to your lesson/unit goals (*Formative Assessments*)?

Feedback Guiding Learning

Conducting assessments and providing feedback during instruction can be compared with periodically checking on the progress of a Lego structure (see p. 97).

TIP 7

Monitoring, Assessment, and Feedback That Guide and Inform Instruction and Learning

Score	1 (Needs Improvement)	3 (Proficient)	5 (Exemplary)
Feedback Guiding Learning (7a)	**Provides feedback to guide and support student learning.**		
	Teacher feedback is lacking or nonspecific and vague.	Teacher frequently provides specific, focused feedback.	Teacher (and when appropriate, students) consistently provides focused feedback that ties directly to objective(s).
	Teacher feedback is rare or absent and only corrective (right/wrong) when present.	Teacher frequently provides feedback that scaffolds learning.	Additionally, feedback is timely—given at time when students most need it.
Formative Assessments (7b)	**Adjusts instruction based on formative assessment data.**		
	Formative assessments are not evident except for didactic questioning of individual students.	Numerous formative assessments of all students occur during lesson, with formative data guiding instructional decisions.	Additionally, learning is differentiated for students based on formative data; students routinely self-assess to monitor their own learning.
	Prior knowledge is not assessed.	Prior knowledge is assessed at beginning of lesson to identify benchmark ability/ knowledge and relevant misconceptions held.	Prior knowledge/ misconceptions are elicited and clearly used to inform and guide instruction.
	There is no lesson debrief/closure.	Lesson debrief/closure is clearly evident; teacher gathers information from some students to guide the next instructional steps.	Additionally, data are gathered from all to track the degree of understanding.

- Scaffolding involves figuring out how to assemble the knowledge—what pieces to use.
- Formative assessments continually reassess the developing construction to ensure the goals and objectives are being achieved.
- Feedback provides guidance and assistance in regard to any erroneously placed or leftover pieces, or when objectives are not being met.
- Debrief/closure helps make sense of all the pieces as an entity—looking at the completed structure, not just the individual parts.

The feedback we provide should link to other TIPs, such as TIP 5 (Interactive, Thoughtful Learning). How we question and guide interactions and how we create the classroom culture are critical in determining how students receive and respond to feedback. If students don't respect the person giving the feedback, then it becomes detrimental to learning, not helpful. To improve the effectiveness and usefulness of feedback, it must have the following qualities (Sadler, 2008; Shute, 2008):

- Specific (detailing what, how, or why, not just stating correctness)
- Clear (simple, understandable, and detailing where strengths or weaknesses reside)
- Manageable (avoiding cognitive overload by giving too much)
- "Just in time" (as soon as possible after the solution or task is attempted)
- Valued (part of a respectful culture that encourages acceptance of feedback from peers and teacher)

In addition, feedback needs to promote self-regulation or metacognition—to help students understand what they know, what they don't know, and how they need to progress from their current abilities. If our questions are all superficial and low level, then meaningful feedback rarely occurs because our feedback is limited to confirming or refuting correctness ("yes," "no," "great").

It is important to provide opportunities where you and your students can offer meaningful feedback that improves the written and oral expression of all students. Feedback should extend beyond declarative statements. Effective questions from teachers and peers often prompt students to think more deeply about their work: How can you improve the clarity of your ideas in this statement? How have your ideas changed? Can you provide another example to support your claim? What evidence is this based upon? How does this relate to the goal? For learning to occur, a tension of some sort is necessary; a commitment to want to know and understand—what Piaget called a state of disequilibrium (some call this cognitive dissonance). Regardless of the name associated with it, feedback provides the impetus that is often necessary to prod students to move from the status quo in their work, thinking, or ideas to the next, more advanced stage of performance.

? *What are numerous examples from today's lesson of where you provided feedback that was clear, specific, and valued? What evidence do you have that it was valued?*

In many ways, learning is like climbing stairs—each step we climb is a new level of understanding. Some stairs have tall risers and shallow treads, or vice versa. Some stairs fit our natural stride and others require that we chop our step each time. We even climb stairs differently; some of us climb stairs one at a time, others energetically bound up two or three at once.

This analogy takes us back to Vygotsky's zone of proximal development (1978), which I discussed earlier in relation to TIP 6. Here, we can think of the zone as the difference between what we can do alone and what we can do with help from others. Effective teaching challenges students to work just beyond what they are capable of doing alone. The phrase "just beyond" is the key. The size of the stair or the leap from what students can do alone to what they can achieve with others will vary for each student. So the scaffolds provided are a critical way to adjust the level of challenge so that it is most appropriate for each student. Both diagnostic and formative assessments help guide the degree of scaffolding or support that is needed. The same level of support may result in some students feeling bored while others feel overwhelmed. But differentiated scaffolding helps provide differentiated learning for your students. Examples of scaffolds include the following:

- Preteaching or highlighting key ideas with students before they read, to help struggling readers
- Asking targeted yet guiding questions to help students or groups of students through a roadblock in their thinking or learning
- Revisiting prior knowledge or a prior lesson to guide incomplete thinking
- Working a parallel example, at the same level of difficulty and in the same format, with students and then letting them go back and solve the original problem themselves

? *Where did feedback from students or you help to scaffold student learning during today's lesson?*

Formative Assessments

The research has been clear for years: when formative assessments are frequently and effectively used in our daily interactions with students, achievement increases (Black, Harrison, Lee, Marshall, & Wiliam, 2004). This occurs because formative assessment allows us to continually know what our students know and are able to do while also allowing us to adjust instruction based on their needs before we administer summative assessments. Too often teachers fall into the trap of thinking that students understand simply because they have done an activity or been on the receiving end of an informative and detailed lecture. Exposure to a topic or an idea does not equate to deep learning. Formative assessments help us move beyond assumptions toward gathering the evidence necessary to inform and guide our teaching.

All effective formative assessments have two major components: (1) data are gathered from *every* learner, and (2) the teacher adjusts instruction based upon the results of the data. It is common to assume that asking individual students questions during a class discussion is a good method of formative assessment. The discussion may be beneficial, but it is not a formative assessment until all students have been queried.

Examples of formative assessments include formative probes, think-pair-share, jigsaw (individuals are part of "expert" groups and then share with their "home" group), quizzes, fist to five (quick self-assessment of understanding), instant-response systems (clickers), exit slips, and self-assessments. Of all the formative assessments, two tend to be the most informative for me, and I find them quick to do. First, every student gets a simple laminated index card with *A* and *B* on opposite ends of one side and *C* and *D* on opposite ends of the other side. Students can quickly hold up their answer by showing the correct response and covering the incorrect answer with their hand to a multiple choice or true/false (True = A, and False = B) question. No batteries needed; no technology to fail; no start-up time necessary. And it's cheap. My other favorite method is the use of mini white boards. Each student responds on his or her own board, and then all hold up their responses to the question or problem provided. This allows students to draw, write, model, question, or use a combination of responses.

Regardless of the strategy used—and there are many available—effective formative assessments are not graded, are gathered from everyone (not just a few), and are varied. The critical point is to make sure you gather meaningful data from *all* students regularly throughout the learning process. Although the number is somewhat arbitrary, I challenge all teachers to assess formatively at least three times during each class. To be clear, the real power of learning occurs in the formative stages of learning and assessment—not in the summative stage.

? *Where did you check in formatively with all students during today's lesson? What did the data tell you, and how did the data inform your instruction? How often did you check in with all students during today's lesson? What did the assessment data tell you about learning? What decisions did you make based on the data?*

Perhaps one of the most profound, though seemingly simple, statements regarding effective teaching and learning is from David Ausubel (1968), who said, "The most important single factor influencing learning is what the learner already knows. Ascertain this and teach him accordingly" (p. vi). The implication is that there are no limits to learning as long as we continue to link new ideas and learning to prior knowledge.

As educators, we often make assumptions regarding what students know and are able to do, what they struggle with, and what they clearly don't understand. Effective teachers move beyond assumptions and seek evidence to support or refute their intuitions. Assessing students' prior knowledge requires that we check in with all students and not just ask one student during a discussion and assume that the response is indicative of the collective knowledge of all students. Further, when we gather prior knowledge during diagnostic assessments, the goal is not to clarify, correct, or resolve any misconceptions held until later in the lesson when students have first been able to grapple with the content. Rather, the goal is to gain insights into where the instruction needs to go and what needs to be clarified during the instructional sequence.

? *How well do you understand the prior knowledge of all your students relative to the current lesson/unit? How much growth have they currently made—individually and as a class?*

Great orators from Cicero to Nelson Mandela modeled the adage that great presentations include three essential components:

- Tell them what you're going to tell them.
- Tell them.
- Tell them what you told them.

For educators, the goal is not to just "tell them" but rather to engage students in the learning experience whenever possible; so perhaps the three-part message for teachers is better stated as this:

- Provide clear objectives.
- Engage the learner.
- Pull the pieces together.

It is difficult to find a classroom where the objectives are not explicitly stated or written somewhere. Teachers are generally proficient in this first part of the three-part message. Just make sure that learners are clear in what they will be able to do by the end of the lesson—this provides a challenge from the beginning. The second portion, engaging the learner, has been central to several of the previous chapters, such as those covering TIPs 2, 4, 5, and 6. The final component, pulling the pieces together, gets little to no discussion in professional development programs and is rarely evident in the classroom. Specifically, it is rare to see a solid "sense-making" component, debriefing, or other type of lesson closure at the end of a learning session. Observations from 17,000 classrooms (Antonetti & Garver, 2015) affirm this major omission, with less than 1 percent of classrooms providing a closure experience that involved students, beyond the teacher just summarizing what occurred.

? *How did you close or debrief today's lesson with your students? How will you debrief tomorrow's lesson? How do these lesson closures improve learning, and how do they inform future instruction/interactions?*

Actions for TIP 7

To guide your discussions, self-reflection, and next steps, consider the following actions that address the central chapter concepts for TIP 7: *Feedback Guiding Learning* and *Formative Assessments*.

Action: Eliminate Errors, Blunders, and Misconceptions with Purposeful Feedback

Learning tends to occur most in areas where proficiency or mastery is still lacking. Therefore, your instruction needs to probe, challenge, and encourage thoughtful engagement. When you challenge the thinking of others, feedback becomes a natural and necessary element of classroom interactions. In math class, you can begin with a common but incorrect solution path and have students discuss or individually consider where the error or errors occurred and how to correctly solve the problem. In an English class, you can have students investigate poorly written statements or questions, working in pairs to improve the written expression. In both cases, feedback can come from students as well as you. In science, students can analyze the data set generated from a group and the conclusions that were made. Your feedback can take the form of questions such as these: "Does the evidence support the conclusion?" "What other explanations could be made?" "How can you account for _____?" Remember that errors invite opportunities—opportunities for feedback, input, and growth. Whether it is through guiding prompts or examination of poor or incorrect work samples, you can foster collaborative feedback in your classes.

Finally, feedback does not need to focus solely on the negative (the incorrect, the poorly done). You can also use feedback to model or highlight excellence. In all cases, specificity is critical. When your comments lack specificity, students have difficulty identifying what they need to change or knowing what is exemplary. So instead of saying "great," "excellent," or "well done," you can say, "You did a great job of pulling all the ideas together into a succinct conclusion." "Your detail is excellent in each step of the solution, allowing easy verification by others." "I like how you provided four different historical perspectives, instead of one, in the narrative of the events leading up to the Civil War."

? *How can you provide more meaningful feedback to your students in upcoming lessons? How can you work to create a culture where students are willing to share and discuss errors?*

Action: Scaffold Learning with Formative Homework

If homework is a kind of formative assessment, then should it be graded? Probably not, but this places us in a conundrum because students typically won't do homework that isn't graded.

I propose a different approach that encourages learning while maximizing participation. First, have students check their own work (quickly post an answer key). This practice can be a huge time saver if it replaces mindlessly going around the room asking students how they answered each question. While students are checking their work, you can check to see how complete their work is. Then allow students time to talk about areas of struggle or confusion, which can promote meaningful interactions in the class. You can grade homework, but perhaps in a different manner. Students might earn half credit for completion and half for correctness of one or two selected problems. These problems might be similar to those that will appear on any upcoming tests. If students got an incorrect answer, then they would need to explain where their error occurred, provide questions that need to be addressed, or discuss where they are struggling on this concept if they want full credit.

This approach changes the focus of homework so it is no longer a punitive assignment that requires you to spend lots of time grading with no real payoff for students in learning. The new approach requires students to be metacognitive (identify where their errors are occurring and try to put their struggles and challenges in words), and it provides you with invaluable information regarding where students are struggling so that you can adjust instruction, if necessary. If you have students who love to talk and interrupt even though they don't do their homework, then make it a requirement for them to complete their homework before they have a voice in the classroom during the homework review. If students use this as a way to intentionally disengage from class discussions, then you would need to change your policy or thinking because it becomes self-defeating at that point.

? *If you require homework, how can you encourage greater participation? How can you make homework more about learning and less about correctness? How do you avoid having students just give random responses so they get credit for completion?*

Action: Ensure a "Bon Voyage" with Formative Assessments

It would be absurd for the captain of a large passenger ship to point the ship toward the final destination, leave the helm, and return right before the ship pulls into the dock. When you teach without continual formative assessments, you likewise are pointing toward the finish line and expecting that all your students will arrive ready and prepared to demonstrate solid proficiency. Much happens at sea to alter the intended course (e.g., winds, currents, speed, engine power). Similarly, much happens during day-to-day class time to affect or inhibit learning (e.g., misconceptions form, practice time is insufficient, instruction is too abstract, missing skills prevent full success).

Although objectives outline the journey that you promise to take your students on, formative assessments allow you to see how far they have progressed on that journey and to make course corrections, if necessary. Incorporate formative assessment into your daily instruction, trying various strategies to see which ones work best. Do not discard an assessment type or strategy until you have tried it at least three times.

? *How—and how often—are you using formative assessments to improve learning and retention of knowledge and skills? How did you adjust instruction based on what you learned from the formative assessments?*

Action: Choose Assessment Strategies That Maximize Results

Formative assessments offer multiple benefits, but the number and variety of assessments can be overwhelming. Assessment strategies vary in their effect on learning, so to gain the most from them, it is important to focus primarily on those that directly improve student achievement. For instance, in one example, asking students to read material and then take a quiz as a formative assessment resulted in their having 50 percent greater retention one week later than when they read and did not take a quiz (Brown et al., 2014).

In the chapter on TIP 4, I discussed the benefits of another form of formative assessment—interleaving practice—practicing various competencies at the same time, rather than as isolated units. Interleaving practice allows students to scaffold and continually reinforce their learning, which is far more effective than cramming at the end of a unit. Research has shown that interleaving practice is more beneficial than cramming (Bjork et al., 2013; Rohrer & Taylor, 2007).

Another example of a particularly effective formative assessment strategy is self-quizzing, which is far more helpful than simply rereading the text or notes before a quiz or test. It is important to teach students how to quiz themselves or others, because it is a skill that is not inherently possessed and must be learned. Typically, students who are more successful academically have learned or had self-quizzing modeled for them by a parent, sibling, or mentor who helped them prepare for an upcoming test.

Many students resort to cramming for a test, but if the goal is retention of knowledge, better approaches are those suggested here—quizzes to expose where knowledge is solid and where further work is needed, interleaving practice, and self-quizzing and peer quizzing.

? *What are at least 15 to 20 different types of formative assessments that you could use in your classroom? (Consult books or websites for ideas.) Which formative assessments and scaffolds are most beneficial to your students over the long term?*

Action: Get Creative with Approaches to Lesson Closure

An all-too-common closure strategy that many teachers use by default is the exit slip or exit ticket. Although often appropriate, this practice becomes monotonous if used in every class, with every teacher. You want students to make solid connections in their learning, and providing some variety in lesson closure helps to motivate them. Here are some strategies for students that offer creative alternatives to exit slips or tickets:

- *How Tweet!* Create a tweet (140 characters or less) that captures today's lesson. (Based on average word length, a tweet would have about 20 to 23 words, and this technique is a good way to practice conciseness. Just make sure students spend their time writing and not counting characters.)
- *This Just In!* Create a headline for a news story that encapsulates the meaning of the objective/lesson in 12 or fewer words.
- *Past and Present.* Briefly summarize what has changed. Specifically, what did you think in the past and what do you think differently now?
- *Picture This!* Draw an icon, an image, or a cartoon that illustrates the concept with 25 or fewer words for the caption or explanation.
- *Dear Johnny.* Write a postcard (index card) to an absent student (real or fictitious) that describes today's lesson. (This technique is particularly effective when several students were actually absent— the cards can be given to them the next day.)

Although a teacher-led debriefing is sometimes helpful, it is often more beneficial for the students to engage in the metacognitive (thinking about their own thinking) aspects of the debriefing or lesson closure. When you ask them to synthesize, question, or analyze what they have been working on during the lesson, they become more aware of what they know and don't know. When they acknowledge what they don't know, they become more engaged, question more, and study harder.

Remember that debriefing or closure need not always come at the end of the class period, especially because an exploration or explanation often comes well before the class is over. Further, if you typically reserve the end of class time for independent work, then it may be preferable to do the closure activity before students begin working on their own.

? *How do you tend to debrief or close your lessons? How engaged are students (and what do you base your claim on)? What does closure tell you and your students about their progress? How can you vary the closure of lessons and make closure more metacognitive for the students and less about a summary provided by you?*

CONCLUSION

Moving Forward

Yes, we have mandates that have to be addressed. Yes, we are limited in controlling what happens to our students beyond the school walls. But we still have enormous control over the teacher factors that influence student success. These factors are strong enough that, when executed well, they can provide a culture that encourages all students to thrive, succeed, and learn.

Middle and high school teachers have about 180 hours during the school year to achieve significant learning among all their students; elementary teachers have more hours but also have more disciplines to address. Students will forget most of the facts and small details that were presented in a given year, so what endures? What will students take with them after they leave?

Will the enduring elements be recalling multiplication tables, reciting of a Shakespearean sonnet, drawing an accurate representation of the water cycle, or listing five facts from the Neolithic Period? Or will students know how to solve complex problems, be able to discuss what makes literature great, convey the importance of water in sustainable environments, or explain how one culture learns from another? The latter examples do not exclude the importance of knowing facts. Rather, the facts become secondary, instead of primary, drivers of the learning.

This book has sought to challenge you and teachers at your school to think more deeply about what makes teaching and learning effective. The first three TIPs are more foundational yet crucial to success (TIP 1: Coherent, Connected Learning Progression; TIP 2: Strategies, Resources, and Technologies That Enhance Learning; and TIP 3: Safe, Respectful, Well-Organized Learning Environment). The final four TIPs challenge you to improve your interactions, to deepen rigor, and to increase creativity (TIP 4: Challenging, Rigorous Learning Experiences; TIP 5: Interactive, Thoughtful Learning; TIP 6: Creative, Problem-Solving Culture; and TIP 7: Monitoring, Assessment, and Feedback That Guide and Inform Instruction and Learning).

All seven TIPs collectively encourage you to improve the intentionality of your teaching and, ultimately, student success. Highly effective teaching doesn't just happen. It is the result of continual growth, in which tomorrow is a bit better than today—even if today was already pretty good. The degree to which you grow and continue to grow as a teacher is largely up to you.

This book, although it is not intended to be the full solution, provides a major step in helping all teachers move forward if they are receptive to exploring and critiquing their own practice. We should all strive for excellence in the classroom, but the TIPS framework provides clearly targeted steps that all teachers and schools should strive toward as they move toward proficiency and above. TIPS provides more than a checklist; it provides a descriptive rubric that can help guide conversations, encourage the gathering of evidence, and promote a higher standard for what teaching in the 21st century needs to look and feel like.

APPENDIX A

Teacher Intentionality of Practice Scale (TIPS)

The rubrics in this section, as well as the Needs Assessment on pages 9–12, are available as a download at www.ascd.org/ASCD/pdf/books /marshall2016.pdf. Use this unique key code to unlock the files: marshall 117001.

If you have difficulty accessing the files, send an e-mail to webhelp @ascd.org or call 1-800-933-ASCD for assistance.

TIP 1: Coherent, Connected Learning Progression

Score	1 (Needs Improvement)	3 (Proficient)	5 (Exemplary)
Learning Progression (1a)	**Implements sound, coherent learning progression.**		
	Lesson contains content errors, lacks clarity, and aligns poorly with standards, objectives, and assessments.	Lesson is generally clear, logically sequenced, and aligned well to standards, measurable objectives, and assessments. Content taught is accurate.	Lesson is consistently clear, logically sequenced, and aligned well to standards, measurable objectives, and assessments. Content taught is accurate and connected to the students.
	Lesson teaches processes/practices separately from concepts/content.	Lesson integrates practices/processes and knowledge.	Lesson requires students to engage with both processes/practices and concepts/content.
Connectedness of Learning (1b)	**Connects learning to students' lives and big ideas.**		
	No explicit connection is made to big picture within discipline.	Learning is explicitly connected to the bigger picture within the discipline or to other disciplines.	Multiple connections are made throughout the lesson as to how lesson/concepts are connected to bigger picture within the discipline and/or other disciplines.
	No explicit connections are made to students' lives.	Connections are made to link content with students' lives or prior learning.	Connections are rich, vibrant, and linked to students' lives and prior learning. Students are actively involved in making real-world connections.

Overall TIP 1 Score
Feedback/Comments:

TIP 2: Strategies, Resources, and Technologies That Enhance Learning

Score	1 (Needs Improvement)	3 (Proficient)	5 (Exemplary)
Student-Centered Strategies (2a)	**Facilitates learning through student-centered learning approaches.**		
	Strategies and learning are entirely abstract.	Strategies provide concrete experiences and visual means to study abstract concepts and ideas.	Additionally, an explicit link is made to tie the concrete experience with the abstract idea.
	Students are passive learners and instruction focuses mostly on memorization of isolated facts and knowledge.	Students are active learners, engaged during a significant portion of the lesson in ways that support building conceptual understanding.	Students are active learners throughout the lesson and focused on uniting knowledge and skills to promote deep conceptual understanding.
	Learning is only teacher centered and teacher directed.	Instructional strategies are predominantly student centered, requiring more than mimicking or verification of what teacher modeled.	Instructional strategies are solely student centered, requiring more than mimicking or confirmation of what teacher modeled.
Resources and Technologies (2b)	**Provides resources and technologies to support learning.**		
	Materials and resources don't help make abstract ideas concrete for the learner.	Materials and resources provide concrete and visual means to study abstract ideas.	Materials and resources provide multiple ways for learners to concretely and visually study abstract ideas.
	Materials, resources, strategies, and technologies are largely lacking or lack purpose, distract learning, and lack efficiency.	Materials, resources, strategies, and technologies are not overly distractive and are purposeful and, when possible, are an enhancement to learning.	Materials, resources, and strategies are purposeful, and technologies are transformative (allow us to do something that would not otherwise be possible).
Overall TIP 2 Score			
Feedback/Comments:			

TIP 3: Safe, Respectful, Well-Organized Learning Environment			
Score	**1** **(Needs Improvement)**	**3** **(Proficient)**	**5** **(Exemplary)**
Classroom Flow (3a)	**Manages instructional time and noninstructional routines smoothly and effectively.**		
	Teacher has difficulty properly pacing and refocusing class after transitions; lots of non-learning time is wasted.	Pacing and transitions are efficient, smooth, with little time lost during transitions.	Additionally, students typically respond with automaticity to cues during lesson.
	Instructional procedures are disjointed and lack organization. Interruptions and noninstructional tasks significantly consume time.	Instructional procedures are clear, purposeful, and engaging. Any noninstructional interruptions are brief, with students quickly refocusing.	High automaticity in procedures is evident. After interruptions students quickly return to established routines with little to no prompting from teacher.
	Students behave as if unaware or confused regarding basic routines.	Routines flow smoothly, are known by students, and provide little disruption to learning.	Additionally, students are familiar with and respond promptly to routine cues. Classroom appears to "run itself."

TIP 3: Safe, Respectful, Well-Organized Learning Environment—(*continued*)

Score	1 (Needs Improvement)	3 (Proficient)	5 (Exemplary)
Classroom Interactions (3b)	**Manages student behavior effectively; cultivates a respectful and collaborative climate.**		
	Behavior management is lacking or poorly implemented. Student behavior significantly compromises classroom safety and instructional progression.	Behavior management is evident, clearly proactive, and appropriately reactive when necessary.	Additionally, students respond promptly to management expectations—consistently refocusing self and others.
	Teacher displays negative affect and lacks patience.	Teacher conveys solid presence, positive affect, and patience.	Additionally, all students are engaged in creating a positive, respectful environment.
	Teacher appears unapproachable, provides little to no support, is condescending, frequently sarcastic, and/or clearly disrespectful.	Teacher is approachable, supportive, and respectful during interactions.	Teacher demonstrates active support for all learners, and students engage in respectful dialogue with peers.

Overall TIP 3 Score

Feedback/Comments:

TIP 4: Challenging, Rigorous Learning Experiences			
Score	1 (Needs Improvement)	3 (Proficient)	5 (Exemplary)
Culture of Challenge (4a)	Facilitates climate of perseverance and high expectations.		
	Expectations are set low and/or not communicated clearly to students.	Teacher sets and communicates appropriate, high expectations.	Teacher and students collectively pursue high expectations.
	Persistence, perseverance, and self-monitoring are not modeled by teacher or demonstrated by students.	Persistence, perseverance, and/or self-monitoring are modeled by teacher and demonstrated by most students.	Persistence, perseverance, and/or self-monitoring are demonstrated by all students, regardless of ability level.
Instructional Challenge (4b)	Provides challenging, differentiated learning experiences.		
	Lesson is superficial, lacking challenge or rigor.	Lesson provides appropriate challenge.	Lesson provides significant opportunities where all students are appropriately challenged.
	Instruction is uniform in delivery and lacks scaffolding to make learning accessible to most.	Instruction is differentiated and provides appropriate scaffolds to address varied levels of readiness.	Learning is differentiated to challenge all learners, with appropriate scaffolds used to maximize learning.
Overall TIP 4 Score			
Feedback/Comments:			

TIP 5: Interactive, Thoughtful Learning

Score	1 (Needs Improvement)	3 (Proficient)	5 (Exemplary)
Culture of Interactivity (5a)	Promotes culture of rich interactivity.		
	Teacher does not actively involve students in the lesson; student participation is missing or rare.	Questioning stimulates participation and involvement of all students at various points in the lesson.	Questioning stimulates participation and involvement of all students consistently throughout lesson.
	No explicit interactions are facilitated between teacher and students or among peers; instruction discourages conversation, questions, or engagement.	Interactions facilitated are at times conversational, engaging, and/or motivating.	Interactions facilitated are consistently conversational, engaging, and motivating throughout entire lesson.
	All learning is either intrapersonal (individual) or interpersonal (collaborative); no balance seen.	Learning experiences provide balance of interpersonal (collaborative) and intrapersonal (individual) learning.	Additionally, interpersonal and intrapersonal learning is effectively timed and linked to the lesson.
Depth of Engagement (5b)	Facilitates thoughtful, purposeful student engagement.		
	Interactions and assignments lack explicit purpose and personal connection to students.	Interactions and assignments are purposeful (linked to key skills and/or knowledge) and personal (relevant, motivating, engaging to learner).	Additionally, students provide evidence of connections to personal applications through discussion, reflections, or other observable data.
	Interactions focus on one correct answer; typically short-answer responses are expected.	Interactions frequently challenge students to explain, reason, and/or justify thinking and solutions.	Additionally, students frequently critique the responses of other students and the teacher.
Overall TIP 5 Score			
Feedback/Comments:			

TIP 6: Creative, Problem-Solving Culture

Score	1 (Needs Improvement)	3 (Proficient)	5 (Exemplary)
Creative Culture (6a)	**Fosters creative, inquisitive learning environment.**		
	Students are expected to give knowledge back in same form it was presented.	Creativity in expressing thoughts and ideas is encouraged. Teacher models creative approaches.	Students are expected to find novel ways to communicate, share, present, and/or discuss ideas and are praised for doing so.
	Student curiosity and questioning are stifled by teacher actions.	Culture perpetuates and encourages student curiosity and questioning.	Curiosity and questioning are prevalent during multiple aspects of the lesson.
Problem-Solving Environment (6b)	**Provides learning experiences that encourage creativity and problem solving.**		
	No open-ended problems are studied. Students only learn to mimic teacher.	Teacher creates environment where students seek solutions to open-ended problems.	Additionally, students are fairly self-directed in their quest for solutions, and open-ended problems are complex and/or multi-stepped.
	Lesson focuses on single perspective/ solution with no student creativity allowed or encouraged.	Teacher presents lessons that provide opportunities for considering multiple perspectives and alternate solutions/explanations.	Students actively consider multiple perspectives and offer alternative solutions/ explanations without teacher prompting.
	Everything is defined/ told before students explore/question/ observe (algorithm, definitions, or explanation all precede experience); or there is no exploration at all.	Teacher facilitates student exploration of major concepts/ideas before formal explanation occurs.	Additionally, students take active role in designing how the exploration will occur.
Overall TIP 6 Score			
Feedback/Comments:			

TIP 7: Monitoring, Assessment, and Feedback That Guide and Inform Instruction and Learning

Score	1 (Needs Improvement)	3 (Proficient)	5 (Exemplary)
Feedback Guiding Learning (7a)	**Provides feedback to guide and support student learning.**		
	Teacher feedback is lacking or nonspecific and vague.	Teacher frequently provides specific, focused feedback.	Teacher (and when appropriate, students) consistently provides focused feedback that ties directly to objective(s).
	Teacher feedback is rare or absent and only corrective (right/wrong) when present.	Teacher frequently provides feedback that scaffolds learning.	Additionally, feedback is timely—given at time when students most need it.
Formative Assessments (7b)	**Adjusts instruction based on formative assessment data.**		
	Formative assessments are not evident except for didactic questioning of individual students.	Numerous formative assessments of all students occur during lesson, with formative data guiding instructional decisions.	Additionally, learning is differentiated for students based on formative data; students routinely self-assess to monitor their own learning.
	Prior knowledge is not assessed.	Prior knowledge is assessed at beginning of lesson to identify benchmark ability/ knowledge and relevant misconceptions held.	Prior knowledge/ misconceptions are elicited and clearly used to inform and guide instruction.
	There is no lesson debrief/closure.	Lesson debrief/closure is clearly evident; teacher gathers information from some students to guide the next instructional steps.	Additionally, data are gathered from all to track the degree of understanding.
Overall TIP 7 Score			
Feedback/Comments:			

APPENDIX B

Resources and Bibliography

Sometimes we are clear on our needs but don't know where to go to find answers, direction, or focus to address those needs. Here are lists of resources that will be helpful as you begin to concentrate your professional development on one or more of the 7 TIPs. These are books and articles that I have found to be insightful, informative, and challenging to my thinking. I encourage you to become familiar with all of them, if possible; but to prioritize your reading, first ask yourself what your most critical needs are and how one or more of these might help to address them. In the lists for the individual TIPs, titles followed by an asterisk are applicable to more than one TIP. The bibliography that appears at the end of this appendix provides more complete publication information for the resources.

Resources

These are books that I feel all leaders and educators should be familiar with:

- *Mindset* (Dweck, 2006)
- *How People Learn* (Bransford, Brown, & Cocking, 2000)
- *Understanding by Design* (Wiggins & McTighe, 2005)
- *The Passionate Teacher* (Fried, 2001)
- *How We Think* (Dewey, 1910)
- *Horace's School* (Sizer, 1992)
- *Drive* (Pink, 2009)
- *The Tipping Point* (Gladwell, 2000)

TIP 1: Coherent, Connected Learning Progression
- *The Teaching for Understanding Guide* (Blythe, 1998)*
- *Understanding by Design* (Wiggins & McTighe, 2005)
- *Essential Questions* (McTighe & Wiggins, 2013)

TIP 2: Strategies, Resources, and Technologies That Enhance Learning
- *Succeeding with Inquiry in Science and Math Classrooms* (Marshall, 2013)*
- *Making Thinking Visible* (Ritchhart, Church, & Morrison, 2011)*
- *The Teaching for Understanding Guide* (Blythe, 1998)*
- "Effective, sustained inquiry-based instruction promotes higher science proficiency among all groups: A 5-year analysis." (Research that justifies the importance of inquiry and shows the achievement gap can be narrowed) (Marshall & Alston, 2014)
- *The Organized Mind* (Levitin, 2014)*

TIP 3: Safe, Respectful, Well-Organized Learning Environment
- *The First Days of School* (Wong & Wong, 1998)
- *Teaching with Love and Logic* (Fay & Funk, 1998)
- *Discipline with Dignity* (Curwin, 2008)
- *Classroom Management That Works* (Marzano, 2003)

TIP 4: Challenging, Rigorous Learning Experiences
- *The Differentiated Classroom: Responding to the Needs of All Learners* (Tomlinson, 2014)
- *Make It Stick: The Science of Successful Learning* (Brown, Roediger III, & McDaniel, 2014)
- *Finding Flow* (Csikszentmihalyi, 1997)
- *Integrating Differentiated Instruction and Understanding by Design* (Tomlinson & McTighe, 2003)

TIP 5: Interactive, Thoughtful Learning
- *17,000 Classroom Visits Can't Be Wrong* (Antonetti & Garver, 2015)*
- *Succeeding with Inquiry in Science and Math Classrooms* (Marshall, 2013)*
- *Asking the Right Questions: A Guide to Critical Thinking* (Browne & Keeley, 2015)
- *Quiet* (Cain, 2013)

TIP 6: Creative, Problem-Solving Culture
- *Making Thinking Visible* (Ritchhart et al., 2011)*
- *The Organized Mind* (Levitin, 2014)*
- *Curious: The Desire to Know and Why Your Future Depends on It* (Leslie, 2014)
- *Sparking Student Creativity* (Drapeau, 2014)
- *Learning and Leading with Habits of Mind* (Costa & Kallick, 2008)

TIP 7: Monitoring, Assessment, and Feedback That Guide and Inform Instruction and Learning
- *Brain-Friendly Assessments* (Sousa, 2015)
- *Visible Learning* (Hattie, 2009)
- *Science Formative Assessment* (Keeley, 2008) (The resource can easily be adapted for any discipline.)
- *17,000 Classroom Visits Can't Be Wrong* (Antonetti & Garver, 2015)*
- *Grading Smarter, Not Harder* (Dueck, 2014)

Bibliography

Antonetti, J. V., & Garver, J. R. (2015). *17,000 classroom visits can't be wrong: Strategies that engage students, promote active learning, and boost achievement.* Alexandria, VA: ASCD.

Blythe, T. (1998). *The teaching for understanding guide.* San Francisco, CA: Jossey-Bass.

Bransford, J. D., Brown, A. L., & Cocking, R. R. (2000). *How people learn: Brain, mind, experience, and school,* expanded edition. Washington, DC: National Academies Press.

Brown, P. C., Roediger III, H. L., & McDaniel, M. A. (2014). *Make it stick: The science of successful learning.* Cambridge, MA: Belknap Press of Harvard University Press.

Browne, M. N., & Keeley, S. M. (2015). *Asking the right questions: A guide to critical thinking* (11th ed.). Boston, MA: Pearson.

Cain, S. (2013). *Quiet: The power of introverts in a world that can't stop talking.* New York: Random House.

Costa, A. L., & Kallick, B. K. (2008). *Learning and leading with habits of mind: 16 essential characteristics for success.* Alexandria, VA: ASCD.

Csikszentmihalyi, M. (1997). *Finding flow.* New York: Basic Books.

Curwin, R. L. (2008). *Discipline with dignity: New challenges, new solutions.* Alexandria, VA: ASCD.

Dewey, J. (1910). *How we think.* Lexington, MA: D.C. Heath.

Drapeau, P. (2014). *Sparking student creativity: Practical ways to promote innovative thinking and problem solving.* Alexandria, VA: ASCD.

Dueck, M. (2014). *Grading smarter, not harder: Assessment strategies that motivate kids and help them learn.* Alexandria, VA: ASCD.

Dweck, C. S. (2006). *Mindset: The new psychology of success.* New York: Ballantine Books.

Fay, J., & Funk, D. (1998). *Teaching with love and logic: Taking control of the classroom.* Golden, CO: Love and Logic Institute.

Fried, R. L. (2001). *The passionate teacher: A practical guide.* Boston: Beacon.

Gladwell, M. (2000). *The tipping point.* New York: Little, Brown.

Hattie, J. (2009). *Visible learning: A synthesis of over 800 meta-analyses relating to achievement.* London: Routledge.

Keeley, P. (2008). *Science formative assessment: 75 practical strategies for linking assessment, instruction, and learning.* Thousand Oaks, CA: Corwin Press.

Leslie, I. (2014). *Curious: The desire to know and why your future depends on it.* New York: Basic Books.

Levitin, D. (2014). *The organized mind: Thinking straight in the age of information overload.* New York: Dutton.

Marshall, J. C. (2013). *Succeeding with inquiry in science and math classrooms.* Alexandria, VA: ASCD & NSTA.

Marshall, J. C., & Alston, D. M. (2014). Effective, sustained inquiry-based instruction promotes higher science proficiency among all groups: A 5-year analysis. *Journal of Science Teacher Education, 25*(7), 807–821. doi: 10.1007/s10972-014-9401-4

Marzano, R. (2003). *Classroom management that works: Research-based strategies for every teacher.* Alexandria, VA: ASCD.

McTighe, J., & Wiggins, G. (2013). *Essential questions: Opening doors to student understanding.* Alexandria, VA: ASCD.

Pink, D. (2009). *Drive: The surprising truth about what motivates us.* New York: Riverhead Books.

Ritchhart, R., Church, M., & Morrison, K. (2011). *Making thinking visible: How to promote engagement, understanding, and independence for all learners.* San Francisco: Jossey-Bass.

Sizer, T. R. (1992). *Horace's school: Redesigning the American high school.* Boston: Houghton Mifflin.

Sousa, D. A. (2015). *Brain-friendly assessments: What they are and how to use them.* West Palm Beach, FL: Learning Sciences International.

Tomlinson, C. A. (2014). *The differentiated classroom: Responding to the needs of all learners* (2nd ed.). Alexandria, VA: ASCD.

Tomlinson, C. A., & McTighe, J. (2003). *Integrating differentiated instruction and understanding by design: Connecting content and kids*. Alexandria, VA: ASCD.

Wiggins, G., & McTighe, J. (2005). *Understanding by design* (expanded 2nd ed.). Alexandria, VA: ASCD.

Wong, H. K., & Wong, R. T. (1998). *The first days of school: How to be an effective teacher*. Mountain View, CA: Harry K. Wong Publications.

References

Antonetti, J. V., & Garver, J. R. (2015). *17,000 classroom visits can't be wrong: Strategies that engage students, promote active learning, and boost achievement*. Alexandria, VA: ASCD.

Ausubel, D. P. (1968). *Educational psychology: A cognitive view*. New York: Holt, Rinehart, & Winston.

Banilower, E. R., Heck, D. J., & Weiss, I. R. (2007). Can professional development make the vision of the standards a reality? The impact of the National Science Foundation's local systemic change through teacher enhancement initiative. *Journal of Research in Science Teaching, 44*(3), 375–395.

Beghetto, R. A., & Kaufman, J. C. (2010). Broadening conceptions of creativity in the classroom. In R. A. Beghetto & J. C. Kaufman (Eds.), *Nurturing creativity in the classroom* (pp. 191–205). New York: Cambridge University.

Benard, B. (2004). *Resiliency: What we have learned*. San Francisco: WestEd.

Bjork, R. A., Dunlosky, J., & Kornell, N. (2013). Self-regulated learning: Beliefs, techniques, and illusions. *Annual Review of Psychology, 64*, 417–444. doi: 10.1146/annurev-psych-113011-143823

Black, P., Harrison, C., Lee, C., Marshall, B., & Wiliam, D. (2004). Working inside the black box: Assessment for learning in the classroom. *Phi Delta Kappan, 86*(1), 8–21.

Brown, P. C., Roediger III, H. L., & McDaniel, M. A. (2014). *Make it stick: The science of successful learning*. Cambridge, MA: Belknap Press of Harvard University Press.

Bybee, R. W., Taylor, J. A., Gardner, A., Van Scotter, P., Powell, J. C., Westbrook, A., & Landes, N. (2006). *The BSCS 5E Instructional Model: Origins, effectiveness, and applications*. Colorado Springs, CO: BSCS.

Cain, S. (2013). *Quiet: The power of introverts in a world that can't stop talking*. New York: Random House.

Csikszentmihalyi, M. (1997). *Finding flow*. New York: Basic Books.

Curwin, R. L. (2008). *Discipline with dignity: New challenges, new solutions*. Alexandria, VA: ASCD.

Darling-Hammond, L., Chung Wei, R., Andree, A., Richardson, N., & Orphanos, S. (2009). *Professional learning in the learning profession: A status report on teacher development in the U.S. and abroad*. Oxford, OH: National Staff Development Council.

Desimone, L. M., Porter, A. C., Garet, M. S., Yoon, K. S., & Birman, B. F. (2002). Effects of professional development on teachers' instruction: Results from a three-year longitudinal study. *Educational Evaluation and Policy Analysis, 24*(2), 81–112.

Dobuzinskis, A. (2014). Los Angeles iPad rollout for schools slowed by technical challenges. Available: http://www.huffingtonpost.com/2014/09/19/los-angeles-schools-ipads_n_5852662.html

Dreifus, C. (2013). Ideas for improving science education in the U.S. Available: http://www.nytimes.com/2013/09/03/science/ideas-for-improving-science-education-in-the-us.html?pagewanted=all&_r=0

Fay, J., & Funk, D. (1998). *Teaching with love and logic: Taking control of the classroom*. Golden, CO: Love and Logic Institute.

Hattie, J. (2009). *Visible learning: A synthesis of over 800 meta-analyses relating to achievement*. London: Routledge.

Howard, R. (Director). (1995). *Apollo 13* [movie]. Universal City, CA: Universal Pictures.

Joyner, R., & Marshall, J. C. (in press). Watch your step! An investigation of carbon footprints. *American Biology Teacher*.

Jung, C. G. (1971). *Psychological types*. Princeton, NJ: Princeton University.

Leslie, I. (2014). *Curious: The desire to know and why your future depends on it*. New York: Basic Books.

Lindgren, J., & Bleicher, R. E. (2005). Learning the Learning Cycle: The differential effect on elementary preservice teachers. *School Science and Mathematics, 105*(2), 61–72.

Marek, E. A., & Cavallo, A. M. L. (1997). *The Learning Cycle: Elementary school science and beyond*. Portsmouth, NH: Heinemann.

Marshall, J. C. (2008). An explanatory framework detailing the process and product of high-quality secondary science practice. *Science Educator, 17*(1), 49–63.

Marshall, J. C. (2013). *Succeeding with inquiry in science and math classrooms*. Alexandria, VA: ASCD & NSTA.

Marshall, J. C., & Alston, D. M. (2014). Effective, sustained inquiry-based instruction promotes higher science proficiency among all groups: A 5-year analysis. *Journal of Science Teacher Education, 25*(7), 807–821. doi: 10.1007/s10972-014-9401-4

Marshall, J. C., Alston, D. M., & Smart, J. B. (2015). TIPS: Teacher Intentionality of Practice Scale. Available: http://www.clemson.edu/hehd/departments/education/centers/iim/research-evaluation/tips.htm.

Marshall, J. C., Horton, B., & Smart, J. (2009). 4E × 2 Instructional Model: Uniting three learning constructs to improve praxis in science and mathematics classrooms. *Journal of Science Teacher Education, 20*(6), 501–516. doi: 10.1007/s10972-008-9114-7

Marshall, J. C., Smart, J B., & Alston, D. M. (2016). *Inquiry-based instruction: A possible solution to improving student learning*. Paper presented at a meeting of Association of Science Teacher Education, Reno, NV.

Marzano, R. (2003). *Classroom management that works: Research-based strategies for every teacher*. Alexandria, VA: ASCD.

McTighe, J., & Wiggins, G. (2013). *Essential questions: Opening doors to student understanding*. Alexandria, VA: ASCD.

Mickelson, R. A. (2003). The academic consequences of desegregation and segregation: Evidence from the Charlotte-Mecklenburg Schools. *North Carolina Law Review, 81*(4), 120–165.

Mischel, W. (2014). *The Marshmallow test: Mastering self-control*. New York: Little, Brown.

Myers, I. B., McCaulley, M. H., Quenk, N. L., & Hammer, A. L. (1998). *MBTI manual: A guide to the development and use of the Myers-Briggs type indicator* (3rd ed.). Palo Alto, CA: Consulting Psychologists Press.

National Board for Professional Teaching Standards. (2006). Making a difference in quality teaching and student achievement. Available: http://www.nbpts.org/resources/research

National Council for the Social Studies. (2013). *The college, career, and civic life (C3) framework for social studies state standards: Guidance for enhancing the rigor of K–12 civics, economics, and history.* Silver Spring, MD: NCSS.

Partnership for 21st Century Skills. (2013). Framework for 21st century learners. Available: http://www.p21.org/overview

Pashler, H., Bain, P. M., Bottge, B. A., Graesser, A., Koedinger, K., McDaniel, M., & Metcalfe, J. (2007). Organizing instruction and study to improve student learning. Available: http://ies.ed.gov/ncee/wwc/pdf/practiceguides/20072004.pdf

Penuel, W. R., Fishman, B. J., Yamaguchi, R., & Gallagher, L. P. (2007). What makes professional development effective? Strategies that foster curriculum implementation. *American Educational Research Journal, 44*(4), 921–958.

Pink, D. (2009). *Drive: The surprising truth about what motivates us.* New York: Riverhead Books.

Plutchik, R. (2001). The nature of emotions. *American Scientist, 89*(4), 344–350.

Rohrer, D., & Taylor, K. (2007). The shuffling of mathematics problems improves learning. *Instructional Science, 35*, 481–498.

Rosenshine, B., & Furst, N. (1971). *Research on teacher performance criteria.* Paper presented at the annual meeting of the American Educational Research Association, New York City.

Sadler, D. R. (2008). Beyond feedback: Developing student capability in complex appraisal. *Assessment & Evaluation in Higher Education, 35*(5), 535–550.

Schlam, T. R., Wilson, N. L., Shoda, Y., Mischel, W., & Ayduk, O. (2013). Preschoolers' delay of gratification predicts their body mass 30 years later. *The Journal of Pediatrics, 162*(1), 90–93. doi: 10.1016/j.jpeds.2012.06.049

Shute, V. J. (2008). Focus on formative feedback. *Review of Educational Research, 78*(1), 153–189.

Thiel, P. (2014). *Zero to one: Notes on startups, or how to build the future.* New York: Crown Business.

Tomlinson, C. A. (2014). *The differentiated classroom: Responding to the needs of all learners* (2nd ed.). Alexandria, VA: ASCD.

Tomlinson, C. A., & McTighe, J. (2003). *Integrating differentiated instruction and understanding by design: Connecting content and kids.* Alexandria, VA: ASCD.

Torrance, E. P. (Ed.). (1987). *Can we teach children to think creatively?* Buffalo, NY: Bearly Limited.

Vygotsky, L. (1978). *Mind in society: The development of higher psychological processes.* Cambridge, MA: Harvard University Press.

Wiggins, G., & McTighe, J. (2005). *Understanding by design* (expanded 2nd ed.). Alexandria, VA: ASCD.

Wong, H. K., & Wong, R. T. (1998). *The first days of school: How to be an effective teacher.* Mountain View, CA: Harry K. Wong.

Yu, A. (2014). Physicists, generals, and CEOs ditch the PowerPoint. *All Tech Considered.* Available: http://www.npr.org/sections/alltechconsidered/2014/03/16/288796805/physicists-generals-and-ceos-agree-ditch-the-powerpoint

Index

The letter *f* following a page number denotes a figure.

About the Author

Jeff C. Marshall is a professor in the Eugene T. Moore School of Education at Clemson University and is the director of the Inquiry in Motion Institute with the mission of facilitating teacher transformation in K–12 mathematics and science classrooms through rigorous and authentic inquiry-based learning experiences.

Among his accomplishments, Marshall received the Presidential Award for Excellence in Mathematics and Science Teaching; he has published 4 books, more than 60 articles, and given more than 130 presentations in the last 10 years. Further, he serves as a consultant for numerous school districts, universities, and grant projects across the United States.

Marshall received a bachelor of science degree from University of Central Oklahoma and his master's degree and doctor of education degree from Indiana University in curriculum and instruction. Marshall can be contacted at 404-A Tillman Hall, Clemson, SC 29634. Phone: 864-656-2059. E-mail: marsha9@clemson.edu.

Related ASCD Resources: Improving Teaching

At the time of publication, the following ASCD resources were available (ASCD stock numbers appear in parentheses). For up-to-date information about ASCD resources, go to www.ascd.org.

ASCD EDge® Group

Exchange ideas and connect with other educators interested in many topics, including Teacher & Principal Evaluation; Effective Feedback; or Motivating Black Males on the social networking site ASCD EDge® at http://ascdedge.ascd .org/

PD Online® Courses

Teach, Reflect, Learn: Building Your Capacity for Success in the Classroom course (#OC004M)

Print Products

The Art and Science of Teaching: A Comprehensive Framework for Effective Instruction by Robert J. Marzano (#107001)

Becoming a Better Teacher: Eight Innovations That Work by Giselle O. Martin-Kniep (#100043)

Building Teachers' Capacity for Success: A Collaborative Approach for Coaches and School Leaders by Pete Hall and Alisa Simeral (#109002)

Changing the Way You Teach: Improving the Way Students Learn by Giselle Martin-Kniep and Joanne Picone-Zocchia (#108001)

Effective Supervision: Supporting the Art and Science of Teaching by Robert J. Marzano, Tony Frontier, and David Livingston (#110019)

Enhancing Professional Practice: A Framework for Teaching, 2nd Edition by Charlotte Danielson (#106034)

The Handbook for Enhancing Professional Practice: Using the Framework for Teaching in Your School by Charlotte Danielson (#106035)

Handbook for Qualities of Effective Teachers by James H. Stronge, Pamela D. Tucker, and Jennifer L. Hindman (#104135)

A Handbook for the Art and Science of Teaching by Robert J. Marzano and John L. Brown (#108049)

Implementing the Framework for Teaching in Enhancing Professional Practice: An ASCD Action Tool by Charlotte Danielson, Darlene Axtell, Paula Bevan, Bernadette Cleland, Candi McKay, Elaine Phillips, and Karyn Wright (#109047)

Qualities of Effective Teachers, 2nd Edition by James H. Stronge (#105156)

Teach, Reflect, Learn: Building Your Capacity for Success in the Classroom by Pete Hall and Alisa Simeral (#115040)

For more information: send e-mail to member@ascd.org; call 1-800-933-2723 or 703-578-9600, press 2; send a fax to 703-575-5400; or write to Information Services, ASCD, 1703 N. Beauregard St., Alexandria, VA 22311-1714 USA.

THE WHOLE CHILD

ASCD's Whole Child approach is an effort to transition from a focus on narrowly defined academic achievement to one that promotes the long-term development and success of all children. Through this approach, ASCD supports educators, families, community members, and policymakers as they move from a vision about educating the whole child to sustainable, collaborative actions.

The Highly Effective Teacher: 7 Classroom-Tested Practices That Foster Student Success relates to the **safe, engaged, supported,** and **challenged tenets.**

WHOLE CHILD
TENETS

1 **HEALTHY**
Each student enters school healthy and learns about and practices a healthy lifestyle.

2 **SAFE**
Each student learns in an environment that is physically and emotionally safe for students and adults.

3 **ENGAGED**
Each student is actively engaged in learning and is connected to the school and broader community.

4 **SUPPORTED**
Each student has access to personalized learning and is supported by qualified, caring adults.

5 **CHALLENGED**
Each student is challenged academically and prepared for success in college or further study and for employment and participation in a global environment.

For more about the Whole Child approach, visit
www.wholechildeducation.org.

LEARN. TEACH. LEAD.